JOHN
for
EVERYONE

PART 2
CHAPTERS 11–21

from Ele

with love

Lw 2002

JOHN
for
EVERYONE

PART 2
CHAPTERS 11–21

TOM
WRIGHT

Published in Great Britain in 2002 by
Society for Promoting Christian Knowledge
Holy Trinity Church
Marylebone Road
London NW1 4DU

British Library Cataloguing-in-Publication Data

A catalogue record for this book is available from the British Library

ISBN 0-281-05520-3

Typeset by Pioneer Associates, Perthshire
Printed in Great Britain at
The University Press, Cambridge

CONTENTS

For

Julian and Miranda,

remembering the great mystery
of Christ and the Church
(Ephesians 5.31–32)

INTRODUCTION

On the very first occasion when someone stood up in public to tell people about Jesus, he made it very clear: this message is for *everyone*.

It was a great day – sometimes called the birthday of the church. The great wind of God's spirit had swept through Jesus' followers and filled them with a new joy and a sense of God's presence and power. Their leader, Peter, who only a few weeks before had been crying like a baby because he'd lied and cursed and denied even knowing Jesus, found himself on his feet explaining to a huge crowd that something had happened which had changed the world for ever. What God had done for him, Peter, he was beginning to do for the whole world: new life, forgiveness, new hope and power were opening up like spring flowers after a long winter. A new age had begun in which the living God was going to do new things in the world – beginning then and there with the individuals who were listening to him. 'This promise is for *you*,' he said, 'and for your children, and for everyone who is far away' (Acts 2.39). It wasn't just for the person standing next to you. It was for everyone.

Within a remarkably short time this came true to such an extent that the young movement spread throughout much of the known world. And one way in which the *everyone* promise worked out was through the writings of the early Christian leaders. These short works – mostly letters and stories about Jesus – were widely circulated and eagerly read. They were never intended for either a religious or intellectual elite. From the very beginning they were meant for everyone.

That is as true today as it was then. Of course, it matters that some people give time and care to the historical evidence, the meaning of the original words (the early Christians wrote in Greek), and the exact and particular force of what different writers were saying about God, Jesus, the world and themselves. This series is based quite closely on that sort of work. But the point of it all is that the message can get out to everyone, especially to people who wouldn't normally read a book with footnotes and Greek words in it. That's the sort of person for whom these books are written. And that's why there's a glossary, in the back, of the key words that you can't really get along without, with a simple description of what they mean. Whenever you see a word in **bold type** in the text, you can go to the back and remind yourself what's going on.

There are of course many translations of the New Testament available today. The one I offer here is designed for the same kind of reader: one who mightn't necessarily understand the more formal, sometimes even ponderous, tones of some of the standard ones. I have of course tried to keep as close to the original as I can. But my main aim has been to be sure that the words can speak not just to some people, but to everyone.

The gospel of John has always been a favourite for many. At one level it is the simplest of all the gospels; at another level it is the most profound. It gives the appearance of being written by someone who was a very close friend of Jesus, and who spent the rest of his life mulling over, more and more deeply, what Jesus had done and said and achieved, praying it through from every angle, and helping others to understand it. Countless people down the centuries have found that, through reading this gospel, the figure of Jesus becomes real for them, full of warmth and light and promise. It is, in fact, one of the great books in the literature of the world; and part of its greatness is the way it reveals its secrets not just to high-flown learning, but to those who come to it with humility and hope. So here it is: John for everyone!

Tom Wright

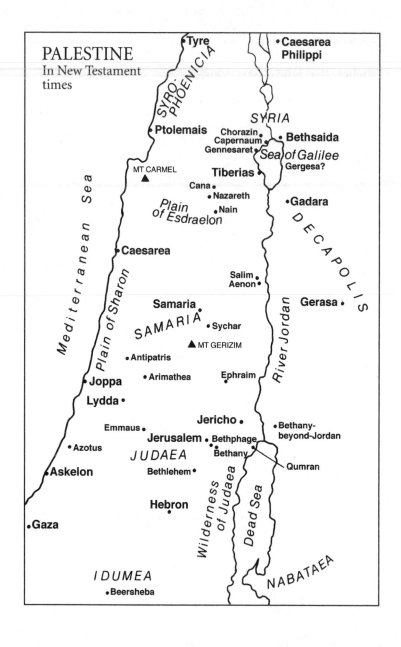

PALESTINE
In New Testament times

Tyre
Caesarea Philippi
SYRO-PHOENICIA
SYRIA
Ptolemais
Chorazin
Capernaum
Gennesaret
Bethsaida
Sea of Galilee
Gergesa?
MT CARMEL
Tiberias
Cana
Nazareth
Nain
Gadara
Plain of Esdraelon
DECAPOLIS
Mediterranean Sea
Caesarea
Salim
Aenon
Gerasa
Plain of Sharon
Samaria
SAMARIA
Sychar
MT GERIZIM
River Jordan
Antipatris
Arimathea
Ephraim
Joppa
Lydda
Jericho
Bethany-beyond-Jordan
Emmaus
Jerusalem
Bethphage
Azotus
Bethany
Qumran
JUDAEA
Bethlehem
Askelon
Wilderness of Judaea
Dead Sea
Hebron
Gaza
IDUMEA
NABATAEA
Beersheba

JOHN 11.1–16

The Death of Lazarus

[1]There was a man in Bethany named Lazarus, and he became ill. Bethany was the village of Mary and her sister Martha. ([2]This was the Mary who anointed the Lord with myrrh, and wiped his feet with her hair; Lazarus, who was ill, was her brother.)

[3]So the sisters sent messengers to Jesus.

'Master,' they said, 'the man you love is ill.'

[4]When Jesus got the message, he said, 'This illness won't lead to death. It's all about the glory of God! The son of God will be glorified through it.'

[5]Now Jesus loved Martha, and her sister, and Lazarus. [6]So when he heard that he was ill, he stayed where he was, to begin with, for two days.

[7]Then, after that, he said to the disciples, 'Let's go back to Judaea.'

[8]'Teacher,' replied the disciples, 'the Judaeans were trying to stone you just now! Surely you don't want to go back *there*!'

[9]'There are twelve hours in the day, aren't there?' replied Jesus. 'If you walk in the day, you won't trip up, because you'll see the light of this world. [10]But if anyone walks in the night, they will trip up, because there is no light in them.'

[11]When he had said this, Jesus added: 'Our friend Lazarus has fallen asleep. But I'm going to wake him up.'

[12]'Master,' replied the disciples, 'if he's asleep, he'll be all right.'

([13]They thought he was referring to ordinary sleep; but Jesus had in fact been speaking of his death.)

[14]Then Jesus spoke to them plainly.

'Lazarus', he said, 'is dead. [15]Actually, I'm glad I wasn't there, for your sakes; it will help your faith. But let's go to him.'

[16]Thomas, whose name was the Twin, addressed the other disciples.

'Let's go too,' he said. 'We may as well die with him.'

Why didn't they *do* something?

A friend of mine had been invited to take on the leadership of a vibrant, growing church. He and his family were eager to go and meet this new challenge. But the church authorities seemed to be dragging their feet about where he was going to live. The present house was quite unsuitable; should they build a new one? Should they convert an existing church building? Should they house him some way off for the time being and hope something would turn up?

Meanwhile suitable houses, near the church, were coming on the market, and nothing was being done. My friend and his family prayed about it, and still nothing happened. I and others prayed about it, wrote letters, made phone calls, and still nothing happened. The time came for him to be installed at the church; it was a great occasion, but still nothing definite had happened. Finally, as the whole church prayed about what was to be done, the log-jam burst. The decision was made. And one of the most suitable houses, which they had looked at from the beginning, had now come down in price. The church authorities bought it, the family moved in and the new ministry began.

But I shan't forget the months of frustration, during which it seemed as though nothing was happening. It seemed as though God was ignoring our prayers for the proper solution. We all got tired of it. People became irritable and wondered if we'd made some mistake somewhere. And I know that there are many stories like that which don't have a happy ending at all, or not yet. In many ways the story of the world is like that. We pray for justice and peace, for prosperity and harmony between nations and races. And still it hasn't happened.

God doesn't play games with us. Of that I am quite sure. And yet his ways are not our ways. His timing is not our timing. One of the most striking reminders of this is in verse 6 of the present passage. When Jesus got the message from the two sisters, the cry for help, the emergency-come-quickly appeal, *he stayed where he was for two days*. He didn't even mention it to the **disciples**. He didn't make preparations to go. He didn't send messages back to say 'We're on our way'. He just stayed there. And Mary and Martha, in Bethany, watched their beloved brother die.

What was Jesus doing? From the rest of the story, I think we can tell. He was praying. He was wrestling with the father's will. The disciples were quite right (verse 8): the Judaeans had been wanting to stone him, and surely he wouldn't think of going back just yet? Bethany was and is a small town just two miles or so from Jerusalem, on the eastern slopes of the Mount of Olives. Once you're there, you're within easy reach of the holy city. And who knows what would happen this time.

It's important to realize that this wonderful story about Lazarus, one of the most powerful and moving in the whole Bible, is not just about Lazarus. It's also about Jesus. The chapter begins with the disciples warning Jesus not to go back to Judaea; it ends with the **high priest** declaring that one man must die for the people (verse 50). And when Jesus thanks the father that he has heard his prayer (verses 41–42), I think he's referring to the prayers he prayed during those two strange, silent days in the wilderness across the Jordan (10.40). He was praying for Lazarus, but he was also praying for wisdom and guidance as to his own plans and movements. Somehow the two were bound up together. What Jesus was going to do for Lazarus would be, on the one hand, a principal reason why the authorities would want him out of the way (verses 45–53). But it would be, on the other hand, the most powerful sign yet, in the sequence of 'signs' that marks our progression through this **gospel**, of what Jesus' life and work was all about, and of how in particular it would reach its climactic resolution.

The time of waiting, therefore, was vital. As so often, Jesus needed to be in prayer, exploring the father's will in that intimacy and union of which he often spoke. Only then would he act – not in the way Mary and Martha had wanted him to do, but in a manner beyond their wildest dreams.

The word 'Beth-any' means, literally, 'the house of the poor'. There is some evidence that it was just that: a place where poor, needy and sick people could be cared for, a kind of hospice a little way outside the city. Jesus had been there before, perhaps several times. He may have had a special affection for the place, and it for him, as he demonstrated again and again his own care for those in need, and assured them of the promise of the **kingdom** in which the poor would celebrate and the sick be healed. John points us on, in verse 2, to the moment which he will later describe (12.1–8), when Mary poured expensive perfume on Jesus' feet and provoked a fuss about why it hadn't been given to the poor. Extravagance doesn't go down well in a poor-house.

But this story is all about the ways in which Jesus surprises people and overturns their expectations. He didn't go when the sisters asked him. He did eventually go, although the disciples warned him not to. He spoke about 'sleep', meaning death, and the disciples thought he meant ordinary sleep. And, in the middle (verse 9), he told them in a strange little saying that people who walk in the daytime don't trip up, but people who walk around in the darkness do. What did he mean?

He seems to have meant that the only way to know where you were going was to follow him. If you try to steer your course by your own understanding, you'll trip up, because you'll be in the dark. But if you stick close to him, and see the situation from his point of view, then, even if it means days and perhaps years of puzzlement, wondering why nothing seems to be happening, you will come out at the right place in the end.

The end of the passage introduces us to one of John's great minor characters. Thomas is loyal, dogged, slow to understand things, but determined to go on putting one foot in front of another at Jesus' command. Now he speaks words heavy with foreboding for what's to come: 'Let's go too, and die with him.' They don't die with him, of course, or not yet, but this is certainly the right response. There is a great deal that we don't understand, and our hopes and plans often get thwarted. But if we go with Jesus, even if it's into the jaws of death, we will be walking in the light, whereas if we press ahead arrogantly with our own plans and ambitions we are bound to trip up.

JOHN 11.17–27

The Resurrection and the Life

[17]So when Jesus arrived, he found that Lazarus had already been in the tomb for four days. [18]Bethany was near Jerusalem, about two miles away. [19]Many of the Judaeans had come to Martha and Mary to console them about their brother.

[20]When Martha heard that Jesus had arrived, she went to meet him. Mary, meanwhile, stayed sitting at home.

[21]'Master!' said Martha to Jesus. 'If only you'd been here! Then my brother wouldn't have died! [22]But even now I know that God will give you whatever you ask.'

[23]'Your brother will rise again,' replied Jesus.

[24]'I know he'll rise again,' said Martha, 'in the resurrection on the last day.'

[25]'I am the resurrection and the life,' replied Jesus. 'Anyone who believes in me will live, even if they die. [26]And anyone who lives and believes in me will never, ever die. Do you believe this?'

[27]'Yes, master,' she said. 'This is what I've come to believe: that you are the Messiah, the son of God, the one who was to come into the world.'

When did you last say 'If only . . .'?

If only he hadn't stepped out in front of that car . . .

If only she had worked a bit harder and not failed the exam . . . .

If only a different president had been elected last time round . . .

If only we hadn't decided to go on holiday that very week . . .

And whatever it is, you will know the sickening sense of wanting to turn the clock back. That's why movies are made, like that *Back to the Future* series, in which people do just that, moving this way and that within the long history of time, changing something in a previous generation which will mean that now everything in the present – and the future – can be different. And of course it's a wistful dream. It's a kind of nostalgia, not for the past as it was, but for the present that could have been, *if only* the past had just been a little bit different. Like all nostalgia, it's a bitter–sweet feeling, caressing the moment that might have been, while knowing it's all fantasy.

All of that and more is here (verse 21) in Martha's 'if only' to Jesus. She knows that if Jesus had been there he would have cured Lazarus. And she probably knows, too, that it had taken Jesus at least two days longer to get there than she had hoped. Lazarus, as we discover later, has already been dead for three days, but perhaps . . . he might just have made it . . . if only . . .

Jesus' reply to her, and the conversation they then have, show that the 'back to the future' idea isn't entirely a moviemaker's fantasy. Instead of looking at the past, and dreaming about what might have been (but now can't be), he invites her to look to the future. Then, having looked to the future, he asks her to imagine that the future is suddenly brought forwards into the present. This, in fact, is central to all early Christian beliefs about Jesus, and the present passage makes the point as clearly and vividly as anywhere in the whole New Testament.

First, he points her to the future. 'Your brother will rise again.' She knows, as well as Jesus does, that this is standard

6

Jewish teaching. (Some Jews, particularly the **Sadducees**, didn't believe in a future **resurrection**, but at this period most Jews did, following Daniel 12.3 and other key Old Testament passages.) They shared the vision of Isaiah 65 and 66: a vision of new **heavens** and new earth, God's whole new world, a world like ours only with its beauty and power enhanced and its pain, ugliness and grief abolished. Within that new world, they believed, all God's people from ancient times to the present would be given new bodies, to share and relish the **life** of the new creation.

Martha believes this, but her rather flat response in verse 24 shows that it isn't at the moment very comforting. But she isn't prepared for Jesus' response. The future has burst into the present. The new creation, and with it the resurrection, has come forward from the end of time into the middle of time. Jesus has not just come, as we sometimes say or sing, 'from heaven to earth'; it is equally true to say that he has come from God's future into the present, into the mess and muddle of the world we know. 'I am the resurrection and the life,' he says. 'Resurrection' isn't just a doctrine. It isn't just a future fact. It's a *person*, and here he is standing in front of Martha, teasing her to make the huge jump of trust and hope.

He is challenging her, urging her, to exchange her 'if only . . .' for an 'if Jesus . . . '.

If Jesus is who she is coming to believe he is . . .

If Jesus is the **Messiah**, the one who was promised by the prophets, the one who was to come into the world . . .

If he is God's own son, the one in whom the living God is strangely and newly present . . .

If he is resurrection-in-person, life-come-to-life . . .

The story breaks off at this point, keeping us in suspense while Martha goes to get her sister. But this suspense – John is, after all, a master storyteller – is designed not least to give us space to think the same questions through for ourselves. This is one of those stories in which it's not difficult to place ourselves among the characters.

Martha is the active, busy one (see Luke 10.38–42), and Mary the quieter. We shall see Mary's response presently. Martha had to hurry off to meet Jesus and confront him directly. Many of us are like that; we can't wait, we must tell Jesus what we think of him and his strange ways. If you're like that, and if you have an 'if only' in your heart or mind right now, put yourself in Martha's shoes. Run off to meet Jesus. Tell him the problem. Ask him why he didn't come sooner, why he allowed that awful thing to happen.

And then be prepared for a surprising response. I can't predict what the response will be, for the very good reason that it is always, always a surprise. But I do know the shape that it will take. Jesus will meet your problem with some new part of God's future that can and will burst into your present time, into the mess and grief, with good news, with hope, with new possibilities.

And the key to it all, now as then, is **faith**. Jesus is bringing God's new world to birth; but it doesn't happen automatically. It doesn't just sweep everyone along with it, willy-nilly. The key to sharing the new world is faith: believing in Jesus, trusting that he is God's Messiah, the one coming into the world, into our world, into our pain and sorrow and death.

JOHN 11.28–37

Jesus Goes to the Tomb

[28]With these words, Martha went back and called her sister Mary.

'The teacher has come,' she said to her privately, 'and he's asking for you.'

[29]When she heard that, she got up quickly and went to him. [30]Jesus hadn't yet got into the village. He was still in the place where Martha had met him.

³¹The Judaeans who were in the house with Mary, consoling her, saw her get up quickly and go out. They guessed that she was going to the tomb to weep there, and they followed her.

³²When Mary came to where Jesus was, she saw him and fell down at his feet.

'Master!' she said. 'If only you'd been here, my brother wouldn't have died!'

³³When Jesus saw her crying, and the Judaeans who had come with her crying, he was deeply stirred in his spirit, and very troubled.

³⁴'Where have you laid him?' he asked.

'Master,' they said, 'come and see.'

³⁵Jesus burst into tears.

³⁶'Look,' said the Judaeans, 'see how much he loved him!'

³⁷'Well, yes,' some of them said, 'but he opened the eyes of a blind man, didn't he? Couldn't he have done something to stop this fellow from dying?'

One of the greatest cultural divides in today's world is the different ways in which we do funerals.

In many parts of the world people still mourn their dead in much the same way that they did in Jesus' day. There are processions, carrying the coffin along the streets to the place of burial or cremation. Everyone, particularly the women, cries and wails. There is wild, sad music. The process of grief is well and truly launched. One person's grief communicates to another; it's part of the strange business of being human that when we are with very sad people their sadness infects us even if we don't share their particular grief. (The psychologists would point out that we all carry deep griefs of one sort or another, and these come to the surface when we are with others who have more immediate reason for sorrow.)

In other cultures, not least in the secularized world of the modern West, we have learned to hide our emotions. I well remember visiting an old lady whose husband had died after more than forty years of marriage. She was busying herself with arrangements, making phone calls, sorting out clothes, wondering what she should wear at the funeral. On the day itself she was bright and perky, putting on a good show for her family and friends. She was with us as we went for a cup of tea afterwards, chatting cheerfully, not wanting anyone else to be upset. I couldn't help feeling that the older way, the way of most of the world to this day, is actually kinder. It doesn't do any good to hide grief, or pretend it doesn't exist. When Paul says he doesn't want us to grieve like people who have no hope (1 Thessalonians 4.13) he doesn't mean that he doesn't want us to grieve at all; he means that there are two sorts of grief, a hopeless grief and a hopeful grief. Hopeful grief is still grief. It can still be very, very bitter.

As though to rub this point in, we find Jesus in this passage bursting into tears (verse 35). It's one of the most remarkable moments in the whole **gospel** story. There can be no doubt of its historical truth. Nobody in the early church, venerating Jesus and celebrating his own victory over death, would have invented such a thing. But we shouldn't miss the levels of meaning that John intends us to see within it.

To begin with, we should not rest content, as some older writers did, with treating Jesus' tears as evidence that he was a real human being, not just a divine being 'playing' at being human. That is no doubt true; but nobody in Jesus' world imagined he was anything other than a real, flesh-and-blood human being, with emotions like everyone else's.

Rather, throughout the gospel John is telling us something much more striking; that when we look at Jesus, *not least when we look at Jesus in tears*, we are seeing not just a flesh-and-blood human being but the **Word** made flesh (1.1–14). The Word, through whom the worlds were made, weeps like a baby at the grave of his friend. Only when we stop and ponder this will we understand the full mystery of John's gospel. Only when we put away our high-and-dry pictures of who God is and replace them with pictures in which the Word who is God can cry with the world's crying will we discover what the word 'God' really means.

Jesus bursts into tears at the moment when he sees Mary, and all the Judaeans with her, in tears. 'He has borne our griefs', said the prophet, 'and carried our sorrows' (Isaiah 53.4). Jesus doesn't sweep into the scene (as we might have supposed, and as later Christians inventing such a story would almost certainly have told us) and declare that tears are beside the point, that Lazarus is not dead, only asleep (see Mark 5.39). Even though, as his actions and words will shortly make clear, Jesus has no doubt what he will do, and what his father will do through him, there is no sense of triumphalism, of someone coming in smugly with the secret formula that will show how clever he is. There is, rather, the man of sorrows, acquainted with our grief and pain, sharing and bearing it to the point of tears.

What grief within Jesus' own heart was stirred by the tears of Mary and the crowd? We can only guess. But among those guesses we must place, not a grief for other deaths in the past, but a grief for a death still to come: his own. This passage points us forward to the questions that will be asked at Jesus' own death. Couldn't the man who did so many signs have brought it about that he himself didn't have to die? Couldn't the one who saved so many have in the end saved himself? John is telling us the answer by a thousand hints and images throughout his book. It is only *through* his death, it is only *through* his own sharing of the common fate of humanity, that the world can be saved. There is a line straight on from Jesus' tears in verse 35 to the death in which Jesus will share, not only the grief, but also the doom of the world.

But there is also a hint of what will then follow. 'Where have you laid him?' Jesus asks Mary and the others. 'They have taken away my master,' says Mary Magdalene just a week or two later, 'and I don't know where they have laid him' (20.13). Listen to the echoes between the story of Lazarus and that of Jesus himself. That's part of the reason John has told the story at all. (The other gospels don't have it; some have suggested that they were anxious to protect Lazarus from the sort of unwelcome attention indicated in 12.9–11. Presumably this danger was past by the time John was writing.)

'Come and see,' they respond, as Jesus had responded to the early **disciples**' enquiry as to where he was staying (1.46). It is the simplest of invitations, and yet it goes to the heart of Christian **faith**. 'Come and see,' we say to Jesus, as we lead him, all tears, to the place of our deepest grief and sorrow. 'Come and see,' he says to us in reply, as he leads us through the sorrow to the place where he now dwells in light and love and **resurrection** glory. And, even more evocative (21.12), 'come and have breakfast'. The new day is dawning; and, though where we live the night can be very dark, and the tears very bitter, there is light and joy waiting not far away.

JOHN 11.38–46

The Raising of Lazarus

[38]Jesus was once again deeply troubled within himself. He came to the tomb. It was a cave, and a stone was placed in front of it.

[39]'Take away the stone,' said Jesus.

'But, master,' said Martha, the dead man's sister, 'there'll be a smell! It's the fourth day already!'

[40]'Didn't I tell you', said Jesus, 'that if you believed you would see God's glory?'

[41]So they took the stone away.

Jesus lifted up his eyes.

'Thank you, father,' he said, 'for hearing me! [42]I know you always hear me, but I've said this because of the crowd standing around, so that they may believe that you sent me.'

⁴³With these words, he gave a loud shout: 'Lazarus – come out!'

⁴⁴And the dead man came out. He was tied up, hand and foot, with strips of linen, and his face was wrapped in a cloth.

'Untie him,' said Jesus, 'and let him go.'

⁴⁵The result of all this was that several of the Judaeans who had come to Mary, and who had seen what he had done, believed in him. ⁴⁶But some of them went off to the Pharisees and told them what Jesus had done.

We saw a programme on the television last night about the fossilized remains of what looks like an ancient race of creatures. They seem to be like humans, but much taller. They appear to have been significantly different from any monkeys or apes known to us. Now the archaeologists are teaming up with explorers (all this takes place in some of the remotest mountains of China) to see if these creatures might still exist.

It's an exciting story, and a remarkable prospect. But I am fascinated by the way in which the archaeologists piece together their finds. Here is a fossil which seems to be part of an animal. Here is a bone which might be part of the same animal. Here is a piece of hair, stuck to a rock deep inside a cave, high in the mountains. Could they all go together? Could one of these puzzles explain the others?

The present passage is one of the most dramatic moments in the whole story of Jesus. When Jesus raised Jairus' daughter in Mark 5, he ordered almost everyone out of the room, and when it was over he told them not to tell anyone. Now he stands in front of a large crowd, puts his reputation on the line, and shouts to Lazarus to come out. (The tomb, like many at the time, was clearly a cave, with a large stone across its mouth.)

And the dead man comes out – a heart-stopping moment of shuddering horror and overwhelming joy, mixed together like dark mud and liquid gold. All this is hugely important. If we don't feel its power, and find ourselves driven to awe and thanks and hope, then either we haven't learned to read or we have hearts of stone.

There must have been many other newly buried people Jesus didn't attempt to raise. There is a mystery about this moment which is bound up with the mysterious uniqueness of Jesus' own work. He brought God's love and power into sharp and clear focus in one small place; only then would it go out into the rest of the world. This passage raises these questions for us quite sharply.

But the raising of Lazarus isn't itself the most extraordinary thing about the passage. The most extraordinary thing is what isn't said, but what provides the link between the two puzzles that we are otherwise facing, like the archaeologist trying to put together a fossil and a bone.

To begin with, we have an unanswered comment from Martha. Good old Martha, we think, always fussing and anxious, wanting to do her best, even at a time like this. 'Master,' she says, 'you can't take the stone away! There'll be a smell!' She knows perfectly well that a human body, particularly in a warm climate, will begin to putrefy within at most three days of death. That's why many in that part of the world bury their dead the very first day.

John doesn't have Jesus answer her, except with an oblique comment: if she believes, she will see God's glory. Somehow, what he is going to do will achieve that. But the question remains: what has happened to Lazarus's body? Will it have started to decay?

The other unexplained bit of evidence is what Jesus says when they take the stone away. He doesn't pray that he will now have the power to raise Lazarus. He thanks the father that he has heard him. And he adds an odd little extra sentence about wanting to show the people around that they should believe in him.

14

How do we put these two bits of evidence together and make sense of them?

John has omitted – but surely wants us to understand, and to be struck all the more powerfully for having to work it out – that when they took the stone away from the tomb *there was no smell*. From that moment on, Jesus knew that Lazarus was not dead, or was dead no longer. His body had not begun to decompose. All that was required now would be a word of command, and he would come out, a shuffling, sightless figure, to be unwrapped and released into the world of **life** and light. But we are left pondering how Jesus had got to that point.

There is only one conclusion that we can draw, and it's very striking. In those two silent days the other side of the Jordan (11.6), before he even told the **disciples** of the problem, he was praying: praying that, though Lazarus would die, he would be preserved from corruption; praying that, when eventually they arrived at Bethany, the body in the tomb would be whole and complete, ready to be summoned back into life. And when they took the stone away he knew that his prayer had been answered.

This, of course, raises the other question which looms up behind this story. The disciples warned Jesus that to go back to Judaea again was to court death (11.8). Thomas, gloomily accepting this as inevitable, proposes that they go and die with him (11.16). Jesus, meanwhile, has been praying for a dear and now dead friend, praying that his body will not decay in the days after death and burial, but that he will be ready to come back to life. We cannot but connect the two, the fate of Lazarus and the fate of Jesus. We cannot but suppose that Jesus, in praying for Lazarus and then raising him to life, was aware that he was walking towards his own death, and praying his way into the father's will for what would happen thereafter.

Of course, there are differences. Lazarus came back into ordinary human life. For him, the process of death was simply reversed. He could still become ill again. One day, he too would die (and there were some who wanted to make that happen sooner rather than later, as 12.10 indicates). But the journey Jesus would make would be *through* death and out the other side into a new sort of life. We shall peer into this mystery when we reach the last two chapters of the book.

For the moment, we pause and reflect not only on the power of God but the **faith** and prayer of Jesus. So often we find two or three parts of our life which pose us the same sort of puzzle that we find in this text, things that should go together, but we can't quite see how. We should remember that in this story the unspoken clue to it all was prayer and faith. If Jesus needed to spend time praying and waiting, how much more will we.

JOHN 11.47–57

The Plan of Caiaphas

[47]So the chief priests and the Pharisees called an assembly.

'What are we going to do?' they asked. 'This man is performing lots of signs. [48]If we let him go on like this, everyone is going to believe in him! Then the Romans will come and take away our holy place, and our nation!'

[49]But one of them, Caiaphas, the high priest that year, addressed them.

'You know nothing at all!' he said. [50]'You haven't worked it out! This is what's best for you: let one man die for the people, rather than the whole nation being wiped out.'

[51]He didn't say this of his own accord. Since he was high priest that year, it was a kind of prophecy. It meant that Jesus would die for the nation; [52]and not only for the nation, but to gather together the scattered children of God. [53]So from that day on they plotted how to kill him.

[54]So Jesus didn't go around openly any longer among the Judaeans. He went away from there to the region by the desert, to a town called Ephraim. He stayed there with the disciples.

16

> ⁵⁵The time came for the Judaeans' passover. Lots of people went up to Jerusalem from the countryside, before the passover, to purify themselves. ⁵⁶They were looking for Jesus. As they stood there in the Temple, they were discussing him with one another.
>
> 'What d'you think?' they were saying. 'Do you suppose he won't come to the festival?'
>
> ⁵⁷The chief priests and the Pharisees had given the order that if anyone knew where he was, they should tell them, so that they could arrest him.

We hadn't been in the country very long when we noticed that our host was driving in a strange fashion. At first, being sleepy from the journey, we thought we were just imagining it; but then it became quite unmistakable. He would drive along an ordinary road, and then suddenly take a sharp turn off, go along some narrow back roads, make a few other detours, and then come out again on what, we were sure, was the same road we'd been on in the first place.

Eventually we plucked up the courage to ask him. Why were we taking these odd little detours? What was the problem?

'I thought you were going to ask me sooner or later,' he said ruefully. 'I didn't want to scare you. But the fact is that we're still quite close to the border here. There have been terrorist attacks on isolated cars, especially after dark. So every time I know we're coming near a place where there have been incidents in the past, I take evasive action.'

At once it became clear. What had seemed like strange, even paranoid behaviour was completely explicable in the light of the threat which, until that moment, we hadn't even thought of.

That is the flavour of the meeting called by the chief **priests** and **Pharisees**. This is the first and only time in all four **gospels** where the word 'Romans' is mentioned; and it explains a great deal, not only what was said that day.

The Romans were behind much of the anxiety of the Jews in Jesus' day, both ordinary Jews and their actual and self-appointed leaders. They had taken over more or less the whole Middle East about a century before Jesus' day. There weren't many Roman soldiers about in the ordinary towns and villages, but there were whole legions stationed a few miles north, in Syria, and the governor of Judaea could call on them for help at any time. That had happened in living memory, and thousands of young rebel Jews had been crucified when the army marched in. Though many Jewish leaders longed to be free from this threat, free to order their national life without having to do what Rome said, they greatly preferred the semi-freedom that Rome granted them to the devastation that would follow if a major revolution sprang up.

And they clearly thought that's what would happen if Jesus went any further. Healing blind people (on the **sabbath**, too!) was one thing; but raising the dead, and doing so publicly where a lot of people could scurry back to Jerusalem and tell their friends about it – this was too much. Obviously, they thought, he was gathering support for some kind of prophetic or even **messianic** action, perhaps a march on Jerusalem itself. Once that happened, if the Romans got wind of it they would call up the troops. And that would be the end of any national hope they might still have. As likely as not, it would be the end of the nation itself.

This forecast of the likely political outcome of Jesus' activity is full of irony and paradox. John's reader knows by now that whatever Jesus is doing he isn't mounting a political-style revolution. The shepherd who speaks of giving his life for the sheep is hardly likely to tell those same sheep to take up arms and follow him into battle. The victory Jesus intends to win will be won by self-giving love, not by normal revolutionary means. Yet the authorities are naturally jumpy. They know of plenty of revolutionary movements in recent times, many of which had begun, as Jesus' movement had, in Galilee. They know that they all come to the same thing in the end. Indeed, many of the Pharisees themselves, and perhaps some of the priests too, longed to see Roman rule thrown off. They knew the way their people's minds worked.

At the same time, with the advantage of hindsight we can see that the fear was justified. Less than forty years later, a real, large-scale revolution did indeed spring up, after some abortive previous attempts. The Romans did indeed come and destroy the **Temple**, leaving Jerusalem a smoking ruin and the Jewish people in shreds.

Jesus, it seems, was anxious on his own account to save the sheep from just those wolves. There is a strange coming together between his own sense of the father's vocation (to protect the sheep from the predators, even at the cost of his own life) and the cynical suggestion of Caiaphas that if one person were to die the whole nation might be spared.

John highlights this by pointing out that Caiaphas was after all **high priest** that year. Even his proposal, a matter of cynical politics from top to bottom, could and should be read as a kind of prophecy, a prophecy which followers of Jesus could muse over and make their own. Jesus would indeed die for the nation, executed in the manner reserved for rebel subjects; but this death would not just be for the nation, but (as Jesus indicated in the 'shepherd' discourse (10.16)), for a much larger company: all God's children, wherever they might be on the face of the earth.

This two-level scene – the politicians anxiously plotting a judicial murder, and John interpreting it as a divine prophecy – brings John's slow build-up on the meaning of Jesus' death towards its climax. From the very beginning he has told us that Jesus is the lamb of God (1.29, 36). Jesus has spoken of his own death and **resurrection** in terms of the destruction and rebuilding of the Temple (2.19–21), which chimes in interestingly with our present passage. He has declared that the **son of man** was to be 'lifted up', like the serpent in the wilderness (3.14–15), so that anyone who believes in him could have **eternal life**. He has spoken of giving his own flesh for the life of the world (6.51), and of the shepherd giving his life to save the sheep (10.15–18).

At thé same time, we have seen the build-up of hostility towards Jesus, especially among the leaders in Judaea. Several times they have wanted to arrest him; sometimes, even, to stone him. Now the whole picture comes together. Jesus' sense of vocation on the one hand meets the leaders' sense of anxiety and political calculation on the other. All it will now take is the right opportunity.

And when better than Passover, when the lambs were killed to celebrate God's promise of freedom? John portrays the scene of pilgrims going up to Jerusalem for the festival; but, in the way he describes them and the question they are asking, he wants his readers to ask the question too (much as in 7.1–13). Jesus has gone away into the hill country just outside Jerusalem. 'Ephraim' probably refers to a town about fifteen miles away, where he was safe for the moment. Will he now go up to the festival? Will this be the moment when all the hints and guesses turn into action?

JOHN 12.1–8

Mary and Her Ointment

¹Six days before the Passover, Jesus came to Bethany. Lazarus was there, the man he had raised from the dead. ²So they made a dinner for him there. Martha served, and Lazarus was among the company at table with him.

³Then Mary took a pound of very expensive perfume, made of nard. She anointed Jesus' feet with it, and wiped his feet with her hair. The house was filled with the smell of the perfume.

⁴At this, Judas Iscariot, one of his disciples (the one who was going to betray him), spoke up.

⁵'Why wasn't this ointment sold?' he asked. 'It would have fetched a year's wages! You could have given it to the poor!'

(⁶He didn't say this because he cared for the poor, but because he was a thief. He kept the common purse, and used to help himself to what was in it.)

⁷'Let her alone,' replied Jesus. 'It's all about keeping it for the day of my burial! ⁸You always have the poor with you, but you won't always have me.'

I always hate it when, in a movie or a novel, a social event suddenly becomes tense and fraught. People who write novels and screenplays seem to like them: anger and bitterness bubbling to the surface, family members losing their tempers with each other, and guests looking on in dismay at the collapse of the occasion. For a dramatist, of course, such moments enable all sorts of useful points to be made. The plot can take a new turn. But they make me shudder. A shared meal ought to be a time of support and friendship, not of destruction and violence.

Part of the tragedy of this little scene is that Jesus badly needs and wants his followers to be united at this moment. The rest of the world is plotting against him; his friends might at least have the decency, you might suppose, to stick together and back him! But no. We can feel the tension crackling in the air.

There is the obvious confrontation between Judas and Mary. But even before that, consider the simple words: 'Martha served . . . then Mary took a pound of perfume . . .'

We have met the sisters before – in the previous chapter and at the end of Luke 10. Every word written about them in the **gospels** coheres. They are rounded characters. We feel we know them. Martha, as in Luke, has made a great dinner for Jesus and his followers. Mary, not to be outdone, steals centre stage, not this time simply by sitting at Jesus' feet, but by her apparently outrageous gesture of anointing Jesus' feet and wiping them with her hair. She would need to let it down for the purpose; that's roughly the equivalent, at a modern polite dinner party, of a woman hitching up a long skirt to the top of her thighs. You can imagine the onlookers' reaction. Had she no shame? What was she trying to say – to Jesus, to the onlookers? All sorts of disturbing thoughts must have been flying round the room. There is a peculiar tension in the air, after all the things that Jesus has said and done and the warnings of violence being plotted against him.

We can imagine, in particular, how Martha felt. She may well have thought that Mary had gone over the top this time; but it was Judas who came out and said it. The other **disciples** looked on, quite likely equally embarrassed by Mary's extravagance, by Judas' outburst and by Jesus' strange comment. John is quite clear where the blame lies. Judas, he says, had in any case been helping himself out of the common purse, so his reaction wasn't sincere.

Jesus goes way beyond all this. What he says is difficult to translate, and John may well know that what he's written doesn't make complete sense as it stands. That may be part of the point.

It suggests that Mary had been keeping this expensive perfume to anoint his body after death. In other words, she like Caiaphas may be saying (in her action) more than she knows. Her act of love is a prophetic statement about the fact that before too long Jesus is going to be buried – and buried so hastily that there might not be time for proper anointing, so he'd better have it right away.

It suggests, on the other hand, that Mary *should* now keep it – anything that's left of it – for the day of Jesus' burial; and that this purpose will be more important even than selling it to give to the poor (remember, as we saw earlier, that 'Beth-any' means 'house of the poor'). In other words, even if she hadn't done what she just did, it would still have been appropriate to hang on to it for that all-important occasion.

This is an astonishing statement, granted Jesus' repeated statements about the importance of the poor, and the **kingdom**-blessings that would come on them. The only explanation is that Jesus believed that his coming death would be the action through which the world as a whole, including the world of poverty and all that went with it, would be put to rights. We who live on the other side of his death and **resurrection**, and yet still face a world of poverty, crippling debt and all the evils which follow from them, may find ourselves wondering whether the church has always got its priorities right.

But there is no escaping the challenge posed by the stand-off between Mary and Judas. It is one of those scenes which positively shouts at the reader, 'Where are *you* in this picture?'

Are you with the shameless Mary, worshipping Jesus with everything she's got, risking the wrath of her sister who's doing all the hard work, the anger of the men who perhaps don't quite trust their own feelings when a woman lets her hair down in public, and the sneer of the person who knows the price of everything and the value of nothing?

Or are you with the cautious, prudent, reliable Judas (as he must have seemed to most of them), looking after the meagre resources of a group without steady or settled income, anxious to provide for their needs and still have something left to give to the poor? (This last was a regular preoccupation. When Judas went out at the supper (13.29), the others guessed he might have been going to give something to the poor, even at that solemn moment.) Put aside your natural inclination to distance yourself from Judas. After all, even at that last moment none of the other disciples had suspected him of treachery. Can you see just a glimpse of him as you look in the mirror?

Or are you back in the kitchen with Martha? If so, how do you feel about both Mary and Judas? And how do you feel about Jesus, and what he said?

JOHN 12.9–19

Jesus Enters Jerusalem

9When the great crowd of Judaeans discovered that Jesus was there, they came to Bethany not just because of Jesus, but to see Lazarus, the one he had raised from the dead. 10So the chief priests planned to kill Lazarus as well, 11because many of the Judaeans were leaving their side on account of him, and were believing in Jesus.

12On the next day, the large crowd that had come up for the festival heard that Jesus had come to Jerusalem. 13They took palm branches and went out to meet him.

'Hosanna!' they shouted. 'Welcome in the name of the Lord! Welcome to Israel's king!'

14Jesus found a little donkey and sat on it. As the Bible says,

15Do not fear, daughter Zion!
Look! Your king is coming now;
Sitting on a donkey's colt.

16His disciples didn't understand this to begin with. But when Jesus was glorified, they remembered that these things had been written about him, and that he had done them. 17The crowd that was with him when he called Lazarus out of the tomb, and raised him from the dead, told their story. 18That's why the crowd went out to meet him, because they heard that he had done this sign.

19The Pharisees conferred.

'You see?' they said to each other. 'It's impossible. There's nothing you can do. Look – the world has gone off after him!'

Even now in Western culture most people know what the

symbols mean. If someone went into a deep sleep, then woke to see shops full of stockings filled with presents, they would know it was nearly Christmas. If they woke up to see people with chocolate eggs, they'd know it was nearly Easter. If they opened their eyes to see lots of children going around on a dark evening dressed up as witches (or worse), they would realize it was Hallowe'en.

But supposing you woke up and discovered that everyone was filling stockings with presents *and* eating chocolate eggs? That could be confusing. You might think someone was trying to make a special point, to say something new. And you'd be right. And that's more or less exactly what happened on the day Jesus came into Jerusalem.

It was Passover-time: the great spring festival at the heart of Jewish life, from that day to this. Passover celebrates the **Exodus**, the time when God set his people free from slavery in Egypt, through the **sacrifice** of the lamb and the crossing of the Red Sea. Passover had its own symbolism, and John is soon going to make sure that we know how he thinks Jesus, the lamb of God, fits into all that. But this incident has other meanings as well.

Although it's the wrong time of the year, the symbols of Jesus' entry into Jerusalem go with Hanukkah – which John has already mentioned in 10.22. When Judas Maccabaeus defeated the pagan invaders and cleansed the **Temple** in 164 BC, his followers entered the city waving palm branches in celebration (1 Maccabees 13.51; 2 Maccabees 10.7). Now, even though it's in the spring, not mid-winter when Hanukkah is celebrated, Jesus' followers wave palm branches to welcome him.

We don't have to look far to find out why. Hanukkah was when Judas and his family became kings of Israel. Jesus and his followers were, so to speak, bringing together Hanukkah and Passover. They were saying both that Jesus was the true king, come to claim his throne, and that this was the moment when God would set Israel free once and for all. The ride on the donkey, with its echo (obvious to people who knew their Bibles) of Zechariah 9.9, makes the same point. And John adds other echoes of prophecies and psalms which all point in the same direction. Jesus is the true king, coming at last to set his people free.

John has framed this episode within the continuing story of Lazarus. Jesus has set Lazarus free from nothing less than death itself, and the great crowd that now follows him into the city have come principally because news of this event has galvanized them into action. Not only the Galileans who had come with him, but a great many Judaeans, were joining in the excited celebration. It was this sign, says John (verse 18), that made them put the whole picture together in this way.

This was the last of the 'signs' which Jesus performed during his public ministry. As John will shortly say (12.37), it was this sequence of signs which communicated to both Galileans and Judaeans who Jesus was and what he had come to do. But there is a darker side to this framing of the story. Because Lazarus has become a primary reason for people to believe in Jesus, the chief **priests** want to kill him too. As Jesus will later say, if they persecute the master, they will persecute the servants also (15.20).

The **Pharisees**, like Caiaphas before them, speak a contemptuous word which John intends us to understand in a much more positive sense. In verse 19 they scoff at Jesus and his rag-tag following. Just as in 7.49 they sniffed dismissively at the common crowd ('this rabble that doesn't know the **law**!'), so here they are determined to distance themselves from Jesus' supporters: 'the world has gone off after him'. The tone of voice can be imagined all too easily. They regard themselves as infinitely superior to the common herd of people. They, after all, know the **Torah**, and keep it to exacting standards that most people wouldn't even understand.

But John wants us to hear something else as well, which will then be developed in the next passage. Jesus has come into the world, because God so loved the world (3.16). He has other sheep to find and rescue as well as the lost sheep of Israel (10.16). His death will deliver not only the nation but also the children of God throughout the world (11.52). It is no accident that immediately after this contemptuous statement of the Pharisees, some foreigners approach the **disciples**, wanting to see Jesus – or that Jesus sees this as a sign that the moment is fast approaching when he will complete his work. 'When I am lifted up from the earth,' he says in verse 32, 'I will draw all people to myself.'

That must be our prayer as we read this story and mull it over. Each of us belongs to part of 'the world'. Our part has, most likely, only heard in a limited way of Jesus. It has probably not discovered that he was and is the true king, the true rescuer, the bringer of true freedom. As we watch his progression into Jerusalem, and on to meet his fate, we must ourselves be drawn into the action, and the passion, that awaits him. And we must ourselves become part of the means by which his **message** goes out to the world.

JOHN 12.20–26

The Seed Must Die

²⁰Some Greeks had come up to worship at the festival. ²¹They went to Philip, who was from Bethsaida in Galilee.

'Sir,' they said, 'we would like to see Jesus.'

²²Philip went and told Andrew, and Andrew and Philip went together to tell Jesus.

²³'The time has come,' said Jesus in reply. 'This is the moment for the son of man to be glorified. ²⁴I'm telling you the solemn truth: unless a grain of wheat falls into the earth and dies, it remains all by itself. If it dies, though, it will produce lots of

fruit. [25]If you love your life, you'll lose it. If you hate your life in this world, you'll keep it for eternal life.

[26]'If anyone serves me, they must follow me. Where I am, my servant will be too. If anyone serves me, the father will honour them.'

Every autumn, when I was a boy, we used to collect horse chestnuts. We would watch the trees as the chestnuts started to fall, usually in late September or early October. The prickly, green outer shell would often split; if it didn't, we would slice it open. There, inside, would be a dark brown chestnut, sometimes over an inch in diameter, chunky and shiny. We called them 'conkers'.

They were beautiful objects, smooth to hold and good to look at. You could line up a row of them on a shelf. But that wasn't, of course, what we usually did. We would pierce a hole in the middle of the conker, thread it on a piece of knotted string, and then battle would begin. In a Darwinian 'survival of the fittest', we would test our conkers against each other, swinging them on the string and crashing them into each other until one smashed to pieces. Nothing so subtle as scoring points: it was death or glory, each time. The winner survived to fight another battle.

Only once in my boyhood did I do with a conker what nature intended them for. I took one of my best ones, a large, shiny, splendid object, and instead of taking it to school in my pocket for the day's conker fight, I planted it. I dug a hole, put in some sand and water, and stuffed it down as far as it would go. It seemed a shame at the time. A waste of a fine opportunity. But next spring there was a tiny shoot. The year after, there was the beginning of a small sapling. I haven't been back to see it recently, but if nobody has dug it up there should be a substantial tree there by now. And it will be producing fresh horse chestnuts of its own.

That is the picture Jesus is using here, though to begin with what he says seems very strange. He doesn't seem to be answering the question. Andrew and Philip have come to tell him that there are some Greeks – foreigners, obviously attracted to Israel's God and the Jewish festivals that celebrated his deeds in the past and promises for the future. But instead of saying, 'How wonderful! Bring them here and I'll talk to them!', Jesus goes off into a meditative comment about seeds and plants, about life and death, about servants and masters. Why? What is he saying?

The fullest answer to the question comes in verse 32, in our next section. At that point Jesus declares that, if he is 'lifted up' from the earth, he will draw all people to himself. In other words, if the Greeks want to see him, want to benefit fully from what he's been sent into the world to do, his proper response is to carry on and complete the work the father has given him. Only by this strange vocation will the non-Jewish world, the world of 'Greeks' (much of the known world spoke Greek, so that was a good way of referring to them), come to gain the truest and deepest access to him that God intended. They wouldn't just 'see' him, as they'd asked; they would 'come to' him, in the sense of being drawn by the powerful love of God, drawn into fellowship and new **life**.

So Jesus' strange talk about seeds falling into the ground and dying is in fact the beginning of his answer. Here we see, more clearly than John has showed us up to now, how it is that God will save the world through the death of Jesus – which has been hinted at in so many ways since the very first chapter, most recently in 11.52. Jesus' death will be like sowing a seed into the ground. It will look like a tragedy, the large-scale, fully grown version of the tiny 'tragedy' that a small boy feels at planting one of his largest and best 'conkers' in the ground and never seeing it again. In fact, it will be a triumph: the triumph of God's self-giving love, the love that looks death itself in the face and defeats it by meeting it voluntarily, on behalf not just of Israel but of the whole world, the world represented by these 'Greeks'.

Verse 23, which ties this passage together, shows that we have at last arrived at the moment the whole **gospel** has been moving towards. 'My time hasn't yet come,' says Jesus to Mary in 2.4. 'Nobody arrested him,' says John in 7.30, 'because his time hadn't yet come.' Now Jesus realizes that his time *has* come: the time when the preparation has been completed, and the great event, the final moment of love and liberation, has to take place. The fact that foreigners are asking to see him, here in Jerusalem, functions as a sign, like the first leaf of spring, that shows where we are in God's planned timetable. Now there will be no holding back. Jesus will go forward to meet the moment, with symbolic actions (chapter 13), special teaching (chapters 14—16) and above all prayer (chapter 17).

As he does so, we are aware that he isn't just talking about himself. Although Jesus does what he must do in a unique way, standing alone against the power of sin and death so that the rest of us won't have to, he is also pioneering a route along which his 'servants', his 'followers', must go after him. Perhaps this, too, is part of his challenge both to his followers and to the 'Greeks'. If they really want to 'see' him, to get to know him and understand what he's about for themselves, they must get ready to be 'planted' in the same way, to risk all in his service.

This picture of being 'planted', as we know from Romans 6, was a picture that other early Christians used to explain the meaning of 'dying with Christ' in **baptism** and **faith**. Here, too, the challenge is not without the corresponding promise. 'If anyone serves me, the father will honour them.' The best 'honour' a chestnut can have is not smashing other chestnuts to bits, but being lost underground as a whole new tree emerges. This must be added to the growing list of powerful gospel pictures which John lays before us, for our own prayer and devotion and service.

JOHN 12.27–36

The Hour Has Come

27'Now my heart is troubled,' Jesus went on. 'What am I going to say? "Father, save me from this moment?" No! It was because of this that I came to this moment. 28Father, glorify your name!'

'I have glorified it,' came a voice from heaven, 'and I will glorify it again.'

29'That was thunder!' said the crowd, standing there listening.

'No,' said others. 'It was an angel, talking to him.'

30'That voice came for your sake, not mine,' replied Jesus. 31'Now comes the judgment of this world! Now this world's ruler is going to be thrown out! 32And when I've been lifted up from the earth, I will draw all people to myself.'

33He said this in order to point to the kind of death he was going to die.

34So the crowd spoke to him again.

'We heard in the law', they said, 'that the Messiah will last for ever. How can you say that the son of man must be lifted up? Who is this "son of man"?'

35'The light is among you a little while longer,' replied Jesus. 'Keep walking while you have the light, in case the darkness overcomes you. People who walk in the dark don't know where they're going. 36While you have the light, believe in the light, so that you may be children of light.'

With these words, Jesus went away and hid from them.

As I was walking into my study to begin working on this passage, I was alarmed to hear three loud explosions from the other side of the street. We live close to some important national buildings, and there is always a danger that terrorists will somehow succeed, despite all the security precautions, in placing a bomb there. It's happened before, and it could happen again. At once I rushed to the window and looked out.

To my relief, all I could see was a shower of coloured stars against the black night sky. It was a fireworks display. As I write this, it is going on, louder than ever. I wonder how many other people in the middle of the city jumped nervously at the first bang. Revolution or celebration? It all depends how you interpret the sudden noise.

This passage is one of the few in the New Testament where we are told that there was an actual, audible voice from **heaven**. And it's interesting to see what some people thought. They heard a noise – and they thought it was thunder. Some people, knowing that Jesus had just prayed, thought that perhaps it was an angel answering him. Nobody seems to have said what John clearly believes was the case: it wasn't thunder, it wasn't an angel, it wasn't a bomb, it wasn't a fireworks display. It was God.

Of course, there was no way at the time that anybody could 'prove' this, and we certainly can't do so two thousand years later. The more urgent task is to see what (according to John) the voice said, and the direction the whole conversation, if we can call it that, was taking.

Jesus had just said that the time had come. He had waited for this moment, for whatever sign he needed that he should move ahead to the climax of his brief but dramatic public career. When the Greeks came to the feast and asked to see him, this appears to have indicated to him that the time had arrived. And he was . . .

Proud that he had got to this point? No, I don't think so.

Exhilarated? Yes, so it seems, but that's not the first thing John says.

Ready to meet the moment with head held high? Well, eventually, yes, but that again isn't what John says.

Troubled. Yes: the **Word** that had become flesh, the one in whom the father's own love and power was truly seen, the one

32

who healed the sick, turned water into wine, opened blind eyes and raised Lazarus to **life**: he was troubled. Deeply troubled, troubled right down in his heart.

Is your picture of God big enough for that? Or, when God speaks, do you just think it's thundering?

Jesus was, after all, the Word become *flesh*. Weak flesh, human flesh, flesh that shrank from suffering as we all might. His natural instincts as a flesh-and-blood human being were to say: the time has arrived – and is there some way I can avoid it? The other **gospels** don't show us this side of Jesus, this internal, troubled discussion he has with himself, until we get to the garden of Gethsemane. John has brought it forward so that we see it now, in Jerusalem, before his arrest.

The key to it all, as often in John, is the glory of the father, and the way in which Jesus was totally committed to doing whatever was necessary to bring that glory about. He has come all this way, has prepared the ground, has spoken of the father's will and of how the world is to be saved; and is he now going to ask for a change of plan? His troubled heart knows that there is danger ahead, but also knows that it is *through* that danger, rather than by sliding safely past it, that the glory will shine out to the whole world. 'Father, glorify your name!'

That is the prayer that gets answered by thunder. God has glorified his name – he's done so already, in Jesus' extraordinary public career, in his mighty and loving works. And he will do so again. Be obedient, follow the way and watch.

He will glorify his name: because those who have usurped God's rule in the world, those who have laid it waste and trampled on the poor and exalted themselves as kings, lords and even as gods – all of them are now going to be condemned. 'Now is the judgment of this world! Now the world's ruler is going to be thrown out!' But it won't look like that. This was the language lots of people were expecting. It was the sort of talk you would associate with a would-be **Messiah**. The next

33

thing you knew, he'd be telling you to sharpen your sword and help him attack the Roman garrison beside the **Temple**.

But Jesus wasn't that sort of Messiah. He was aiming to overthrow the kingdom of the world, all right, and replace it with the **kingdom of God**. But the victory was to be of a totally different sort. It was all about his being 'lifted up', exalted – on a pole, like the serpent in the wilderness (3.14–15). That's how the world would be rescued. That's how God, the true God, the God of astonishing, generous love, would be glorified. Swords don't glorify the creator-God. Love does. Self-giving love, best of all.

Jesus' hearers, of course, don't understand him. They hardly ever do, particularly in John's gospel. This must reflect, I think, the memories that the writer, or his informants, had of endless conversations in which Jesus and the Judaeans seemed to be talking at cross purposes. They know from their traditions that the Messiah will reign for ever. (That's what the Bible says, after all. Look at 2 Samuel 7.13–16.) They don't understand Jesus' obscure hints about his own death, about the strange '**son of man**' figure who would be 'lifted up' (3.14; 8.28). John wants us to feel not only Jesus' frustration, as in their understanding they seem so close and yet so far away; he wants us to sense the **disciples**' puzzlement as well. What was Jesus up to? What did he really mean?

The only clue Jesus will give them at the moment is to speak again about light and darkness. The light is with them for a little while longer, and they must stick with it, walk in it and believe in it. So must we.

JOHN 12.37–43

Glory and Blindness

[37]They didn't believe in him, even though he had done so many signs in front of their eyes. [38]This was so that the word

of Isaiah the prophet might be fulfilled:

> Lord, who believed the story we told?
> Your powerful arm – who saw it unveiled?

³⁹That's why they couldn't believe. As Isaiah again put it,

> ⁴⁰He has caused their eyes to be blind,
> and caused their hearts to be hard;
> so they wouldn't see with their eyes,
> or understand with their hearts,
> or turn, so that I could heal them.

⁴¹Isaiah said this because he saw his glory, and spoke about him.

⁴²Even so, however, quite a few of the rulers did believe in him. But, because of the Pharisees, they didn't declare their faith, for fear of being put out of the synagogue. ⁴³This was because they loved the praise of other people more than the praise of God.

It was seven o'clock in the evening when Susan called the family in. She had worked hard all day to prepare this meal, and she was excited, eyes sparkling, on edge to see what they would say. Delicious smells came from the kitchen.

She sat them down at the table. The candlelight twinkled on the silver and glass. She went back to the kitchen and emerged with the first course, a spicy soup she had taken special care over. They began to eat, talking away about what they'd been doing all day. They thanked her politely as she cleared the dishes away, and there was a short pause as she put the finishing touches to the main course. It was a roast pheasant with every possible trimming and sauce, a feast for the eyes as well as the palate. The vegetables to go with it were done exactly right, with clever little touches to make them even more tasty.

She brought it in under a cover, and put it on the table. This was it. This was the moment she'd been waiting for all day. Now they would see what she could do!

Her father was talking to her oldest brother.

'So I said to Geoffrey', he boomed, 'that if that was all he had to say for himself, then I think –'

Her mother was talking to her younger sister.

'And then you'll never guess what we saw in that little shop just next to the station –'

'ALL RIGHT!' said Susan loudly. 'This is it!' And with a flourish (she'd watched a French waiter do it once, on holiday) she lifted the lid.

'– he'd better find himself another job!' said her father.

'– it was the sweetest little hat I've ever seen!' declared her mother.

'Gosh, Susan,' said her younger brother. 'I thought you knew I didn't like pheasant.'

Susan began to carve the bird and distribute the vegetables. She did it mechanically. Her heart had gone strangely cold.

Now supposing, on the seventh day of creation, when God had made the heavens and the earth, there had been a watching audience. Earth and sea coming out of primal mud. Trees, flowers and plants: every colour you can think of, plus a few more. Fish, birds, animals of every kind, everything from whales to woodpeckers. Then, at last, the human race, the crown and glory of it all: male and female, to reflect God's image into the world. God saw everything he'd made, and declared that it was very good. But supposing the onlookers remained unimpressed? Supposing they went on with their conversations? Supposing they objected because that wasn't quite what they'd had in mind? Because it all looked a bit messy and disorganized?

John has been telling us the story of new creation. The 'signs' have been building up: water into wine in chapter 2, the

36

nobleman's son in chapter 4, the healing of the cripple in chapter 5, the bread in the desert in chapter 6, the man born blind in chapter 9, and most recently the raising of Lazarus in chapter 11. And John has hinted, and will say again later (20.30), that Jesus did many, many other 'signs' as well. These six are just the tip of the iceberg, selected to make their individual points about new creation, new dimensions to God's work, new **Exodus**, new **life**, new light. And yet . . .

. . . everyone went on with their conversations. He had done all these things, and they still didn't believe.

As John tells the story of Jesus' spectacular achievements and the people's remarkable lack of interest, his mind goes back to two Old Testament themes. Moses, in Egypt, did a whole string of 'signs' in front of Pharaoh and his courtiers, and still they didn't believe. The only conclusion people could come to was that somehow their hearts had been hardened, so that God's liberation of his people would be all the more dramatic. That is part of the mystery of Exodus chapters 9—12.

Isaiah, faced with the people of Israel in flagrant immorality and rebellion against God, found himself called to speak God's **word** to them, knowing it would only make matters worse. They had become not just like poor-quality Israelites, but like Pharaoh himself! Their eyes were shut, their hearts were hard, and it seemed as though God had made it that way. They were so sunk in their sin and rebellion that the only course for God now would be judgment; even though, as Isaiah saw, through that judgment an extraordinary new work of salvation would emerge. That is part of the mystery of Isaiah chapter 6.

Now John, with both of these terrifying examples in his mind, looks at the Judaeans who saw Jesus' 'signs'. The only explanation he can find for their failure to believe – and for the fear and secrecy of those who did believe – was that something similar had happened. Most of the people were simply hard-hearted. They went on with their own conversations. Or they criticized. Even those who were soft-hearted, who really did believe that Jesus was the **Messiah**, didn't say so, because they were more concerned about what other people would say about them than about what God thought of them.

But John is clear, and we should be clear, that the new creation was indeed going ahead in Jesus. The new Exodus was proceeding faster than anyone realized. The six signs were leading rapidly to a seventh, the moment when all the themes in the **gospel** would come rushing together and leave history stamped for ever with the image of a dying man on a cross, lifted up for all the world to see, opening blind eyes and softening hard hearts with the love of God. The greatest Pharaoh of them all, the power of death itself, was going to do its worst, and suddenly God would give freedom to the whole world.

The challenge for us is unmistakable. Are we just going to go on with our conversations, as God unveils the project he's been working on all this time? Are we going to complain that we wish he'd done something else instead? Are we going to say that we probably believe in it but would rather people didn't know? Or are we going to admit to ourselves and to the watching world that in looking at this Jesus we have seen the glory of God?

JOHN 12.44–50

The Final Challenge

[44]'Anyone who believes in me', shouted Jesus in a loud voice, 'doesn't believe in me, but in the one who sent me! [45]Anyone who sees me sees the one who sent me! [46]I've come into the world as light, so that everyone who believes in me won't need to stay in the dark.

[47]'If anyone hears my words and doesn't keep them, I'm not going to judge them. That wasn't why I came. I came to save the

world, not to judge it. [48]Anyone who rejects me and doesn't hold on to my words has a judge. The word which I have spoken will judge them on the last day.

[49]'I haven't spoken on my own authority. The father who sent me gave me his own command about what I should say and speak. [50]And I know that his command is eternal life. What I speak, then, is what the father has told me to speak.'

One of the oldest clichés in the movie business is the final showdown between the arch-opponents. The hero and the villain have been plotting against one another all through the story. Their allies and helpers have struggled and fought. There have been gains and losses on both sides. But finally, when the audience knows the movie must be nearly over, the other battles and skirmishes fall away and the two central characters face each other for the first time.

We know the story so well, whether it's in the old cowboy-and-Indian tales, the space fantasies or the endless cycles of cops-and-robbers movies. There comes a moment when the issue is clear. One side or the other. Good versus evil. We know how it ought to end, but we're never sure how it's going to get there.

Perhaps one of the reasons this kind of plot keeps coming back, even if the subject-matter is different, is because the greatest story in the world has a moment like that. Here it is.

At least, if you have eyes to see. Of course, there is still to come the moment when Jesus and Pilate look each other in the face; but Pilate isn't the real villain. He's the villain's cat's-paw. Even Caesar in Rome isn't the real villain. The real villain is the darkness itself, the darkness that John has not yet named. The darkness will soon gather itself into a heap and take possession of one of Jesus' own friends. Once '**the satan**' has entered Judas (13.27), we are not surprised when he goes out into the night (13.30).

This moment, at the end of chapter 12, draws together the challenge that, to John's eyes, Jesus has presented to the people of Israel from the very first until now. The light has come into the world, shining in the darkness, and the darkness has not overcome it. The light has been with them, inviting them to make it their own and walk in it, so that they won't stumble. Jesus himself is the light of the world, the one who opens eyes both literal and metaphorical. And he is and does all this because the source of light shines through him. There is light enough for the whole world to see by, but not everyone wants to see; it might, they think, be embarrassing or shaming or too challenging by half.

But for those who choose to remain in the darkness, Jesus has strange words of new challenge and warning. He hasn't come to judge the world. He has come to save it (see 3.17). He has come because God loved the world so much that he didn't send a lowly subordinate; he didn't send a long-distance message; he didn't leave a note in the hope that someone would find it. He loved the world so much that he came in person, in the person of his own son, the **Word** made flesh, so that he could save the world in person. That was and is what Jesus is all about.

But doing this meant that the light would shine more brightly than ever before, and that the shadows it cast would be darker than ever before. When the only light is a murky grey, people can shuffle to and fro from semi-darkness to semi-light without noticing much difference. But when the light shines brightly, even though it has come with the aim of rescuing and healing, of loving people back to **life**, it means that when people choose darkness there can be no question that that is indeed what they have chosen.

The result is sadly clear. When Jesus speaks the words of love, the words of God, the words that would heal the world, people who reject those words will find themselves confronted in the end, not by Jesus himself, but by those very words, the words they have heard, the words they can't pretend they didn't hear. The words themselves will be judges, will rise up and condemn them.

The words will have this power because they are the words which the father himself has instructed Jesus to say. Here, at the final confrontation before Jesus withdraws from the crowds to be with his **disciples** for a last evening, we find once more, drawing together all we have seen so far, the fundamental claim that Jesus was making throughout his career. He was speaking the words God gave him to speak. People who believe him, therefore, are believing in God; people who look at him and see who he truly is are looking, as in a mirror, upon the true reflection of God.

This is such a stupendous claim that people at the time, and people ever since, have doubted whether Jesus could ever have said such things, or even thought them. They have doubted whether John, writing all this, was doing more than constructing a clever theological fiction. They have doubted whether this is more than a rather strange religious fantasy. But, though the historical questions are always open, and proper research into them is always to be encouraged, if John himself is right the real reason for doubt is the shuddering fear that maybe it is after all true. What if Jesus really were the mouthpiece of the living God? What if seeing him really did mean seeing the father? What if hearing his words and not believing them really did mean having those words return as judges at the end?

We do well to ponder all this, to reflect on our own response to John's portrait of the Word made flesh. This is the point in the story when Jesus speaks to the crowds in Jerusalem for the last time. The next time they see him it will be as a prisoner, standing before Pilate. He will be on trial, and his words will be sifted as evidence against him. But the real

41

trial is already under way, here in chapter 12. Jesus is staring into the darkness, and the darkness is staring back. And everyone who reads this chapter must, sooner or later, make up their minds which side they're on.

JOHN 13.1–11

Washing the Disciples' Feet

¹It was before the festival of Passover. Jesus knew that his time had come, the time for him to leave this world and go to the father. He had always loved his own people in the world; now he loved them right through to the end.

²It was supper-time. The devil had already put the idea of betraying him into the heart of Judas, son of Simon Iscariot. ³Jesus knew that the father had given everything into his hands, and that he had come from God and was going to God. ⁴So he got up from the supper-table, took off his clothes, and wrapped a towel around himself. ⁵Then he poured water into a bowl, and began to wash the disciples' feet, and to wipe them with the towel he was wrapped in.

⁶He came to Simon Peter.

'Master,' said Peter, 'what's this? You, washing my feet?'

⁷'You don't understand yet what I'm doing,' replied Jesus, 'but you'll know in good time.'

⁸'I'm not going to have you washing my feet!' said Peter. 'Never!'

'If I don't wash you,' replied Jesus, 'you don't belong to me.'

⁹'All right then, master,' said Simon Peter, 'but not only my feet – wash my hands and my head as well!'

¹⁰'Someone who has washed', said Jesus to him, 'doesn't need to wash again, except for their feet. They are clean all over. And you are clean – but not all of you.'

¹¹Jesus knew, you see, who was going to betray him. That's why he said, 'You are not all clean.'

I had never washed anyone else's feet (bathing my own children doesn't really count) until I went to work in a church where they acted out this scene every Holy Week. On the Thursday, the day before Good Friday, many churches arrange a service where the senior ministers, copying Jesus, wrap themselves in towels and wash the feet of twelve people.

The first time I did it, I had prepared for the service in the usual way. But nothing could have prepared me for the sense of holy intimacy that went with the simple but profound action of washing other people's feet. Feet are very basic things: not pretty, not ugly, just basic. Down to earth, you might say. Washing them is both very mundane (we all have to wash our feet, and we do it so regularly we hardly think about it) and very close and personal. Washing between someone else's toes is an intimate action. It is a moment of tenderness.

All of that – the love, and the down-to-earthness – comes through in this marvellous passage. It is both the beginning and the end: the beginning of the long, slow build-up to Jesus' crucifixion and **resurrection**, and the end, the climax, the goal, of everything Jesus has done so far. 'Now,' says John (verse 1), 'he loved them right through to the end.'

The first three verses form a detailed introduction both to the footwashing scene and to the whole of the rest of the book. Watch how John, like a brilliant artist, fills in the background with three quick strokes of the brush. Understand each of these, and you'll see not only what the footwashing meant but also what Jesus' death and resurrection mean.

First, Passover. We know John well enough by now to know that, when he mentions a Jewish festival, he wants us to understand that Jesus is applying its meaning to himself. Passover has been, from the start of this book, the greatest of the festivals. Jesus is the Passover lamb (1.29, 36). He spoke, at Passover, of the **Temple** being destroyed and rebuilt – meaning his own body (2.19–21). He fed the crowds at Passover-time, and spoke of them feeding on his body and blood (chapter 6).

Now he is back in Jerusalem for a final Passover. John does not describe the meal itself; presumably he supposes that his readers know the story of it well enough from other traditions, and from their regular experience of the **eucharist**. But in this extraordinary scene he explains, just the same, what the meal was all about, and how it pointed on beyond itself to the events of the following day.

Second, Jesus' time had come. We saw in the previous chapter (12.23, 27) how Jesus had seen the moment dawning, the moment for which all his career so far had been preparing. But now John describes this 'time' in a way which goes beyond what has been said so far, and sets up a whole sequence of ideas which Jesus will explore in the coming chapters. It is time – time for Jesus 'to leave this world and go to the father'.

Not simply 'time for Jesus to die', though that is part of what this means. We should not make the mistake many have made, and suppose that Jesus, in this **gospel** or any of the others, simply 'died and went to **heaven**'. John is clear, in 20.17, that after his death Jesus is *first* raised to new **life**, then meets the **disciples**, and only *then* 'goes up to the father'. But it is this complex and completely unexpected sequence of events, the whole thing together, that means he is 'going to the father'. This is what gives new depth and meaning both to the footwashing and the crucifixion. They are the events which form the ladder from this world to the father's world. They are the acted words the eternal **Word** must speak. They are the way home that the **son of God** must take.

Third, and for John still more important, what is now done is done as the action of supreme love. Think back to the 'good shepherd' of chapter 10. The shepherd loves his own sheep, and they love him in return. And the greatest thing the shepherd can do for them is to lay down his life. Now, says John, 'he loved them right through to the end'. Not just with a dogged see-it-through love, though that is there too. He loved

44

them 'to the uttermost'. There was nothing that love could do for them that he did not now do.

All this, astonishingly, is contained simply in the first verse. The second and third, too, prepare the way. First there is Judas, allowing the **devil**'s whispered suggestion to gain a foothold in his imagination. We shall return to this, but notice how evil creeps in between the cracks at the very moment when love is going to the limit. There is nothing cosy or romantic about this scene. It is about love betrayed, not just love portrayed.

But then, in verse 3, we see the full picture. The Word who was with God, the Word who was God, became flesh. He laid aside the clothes of glory, and put on our human nature, in order to wash our feet. He had come from God and was going to God. Here John is very close to Paul in Philippians 2.5–11. And notice that here, as there, the point is not to say, 'Fancy! Despite the fact that he had come from God, he nevertheless washed their feet!' The point is to say, 'No: washing their feet was what he had to do, precisely *because* he had come from God.' The footwashing – and the crucifixion itself, to which it pointed – was Jesus' way of showing who God was and is. Next time Jesus has his clothes changed it will be to reveal him as 'the man', the king (19.5); after that he will be naked on the cross, revealing the father's heart as he gives his life for the world.

The little drama with Peter, misunderstanding yet again what Jesus is up to, is funny on the outside but deeply serious on the inside. Jesus must wash us if we are to belong to him. Yet he has already washed us, in calling us to belong to him (15.3); what we need day by day is the regular washing of those parts of ourselves, our personalities and bodies, which get dusty and dirty.

When Peter objects to Jesus washing him, this reflects his objection (in Mark 8.32 and elsewhere) to Jesus going to the cross. Neither he nor the others have yet understood what it is that Jesus has to do, and why. Keep your eye on Peter as the story moves on, and see what happens to him as a result. And watch and wait for the moment when, in the final puzzled dialogue of the book, Jesus and Peter once more argue it out, looking ahead this time not to Jesus' work as the good shepherd, but to Peter's work as the under-shepherd.

I have on my window sill a small carving, in Palestinian olive wood, of Jesus washing Peter's feet. I bought it last time I was in Jerusalem. But far more important than carvings or paintings is for the world to see Jesus' followers doing what he did. That's what the next passage is about.

JOHN 13.12–20

Like Master, Like Servant

¹²So when he had washed their feet, he put on his clothes and sat down again.

'Do you know what I've done to you?' he asked. ¹³'You call me "teacher", and "master", and you're right. That's what I am. ¹⁴Well, then: if I, as your master and teacher, washed your feet just now, you should wash each other's feet. ¹⁵I've given you a pattern, so that you can do things in the same way that I did.

¹⁶'I'm telling you the solemn truth,' he continued. 'The slave isn't greater than the master. People who are sent are not greater than the person who sends them. ¹⁷If you know these things, God's blessing on you if you do them.

¹⁸'I'm not talking about all of you,' he went on. 'I know the ones I have chosen. What the Bible says has to come true: "The person who ate my bread lifted up his heel against me." ¹⁹I'm telling you this now, before it happens, so that when it does happen you may believe that I am who I am. ²⁰I'm telling you the solemn truth: anyone who welcomes someone I send, welcomes me, and anyone who welcomes me, welcomes the one who sent me.'

I was given a beautiful present this week. To celebrate a special anniversary, someone close to me spent hours and hours weaving a careful tapestry, a needlepoint work of art. The theme comes from one of the early Celtic **gospels**, and is a picture of the four gospel-writers, Matthew, Mark, Luke and John. Each one is accompanied by the particular symbol some early Christians gave them: Matthew by an angel, Mark by a lion, Luke by an ox, and John by an eagle.

I've never done a needlepoint tapestry like that, but I've watched, and I know how it's done. You need the pattern, the outline: someone has to design it, and colour it on to the canvas so that the artist can see which coloured threads go where. Then the pattern has to be followed very carefully, stitch by stitch. It's laborious, and a bit of a strain on the eyes, but as the work develops there is a growing sense of excitement as the picture comes alive, and of anticipation of the complete work. Finally it is framed, ready to be hung on the wall as an object of beauty and interest, a sign (in this case) both of love and of a particular moment.

Jesus speaks in verse 15 of giving his followers a *pattern* to copy. The word he uses could mean, in the ancient world, a picture showing how something was to be done, a tracing that someone else would follow, filling in the details. And this pattern sets Jesus' followers a task so laborious, requiring such a strain not only on the eyes but also on the nerves, will, heart and energy, that we shouldn't be surprised at how many of us fail to get it right. Jesus, having washed his **disciples**' feet, declares that he has established a pattern for them to follow.

Why is this so hard? Why does he have to go on to insist that the slave is not greater than the master, that the person who is sent is not greater than the person who sent them?

Because we are proud. Today, when we perform the foot-washing ceremony in our churches, as I described in the previous section, it is the leader, the senior minister, who does it.

It has become a sign of leadership. When Jesus did it, he was doing what normally a slave would do; but when we do it, we're doing what Jesus did. Though, as I said before, it is a deeply intimate and moving thing to do, it is still, rather obviously, the leader of the congregation copying Jesus – and, in a strange way, having his or her own authority and status enhanced by doing so.

Somehow we need to get beyond this. Thank God there are many Christian leaders who do. Of course, the acting out of the symbol is only the tip of the iceberg. The critical thing is whether the same leader is prepared to get up in the middle of the night to sit beside the bed of an old, frail, frightened man who is dying all alone. The test that matters is whether the same leader is ready, without a word of either complaint or boasting, to stay behind after the meeting and do the washing-up or put out the garbage. Of course, it's important that everybody in a church family helps with the necessary tasks. But the truly Christlike leader is known by the ease and spontaneity with which he or she does the little, annoying, messy things – the things which in the ancient world the slave would do, the things which in our world we always secretly hope someone else will do so we won't have to waste our time, to demean ourselves.

The church needs to learn this again and again, because (God forgive us!) we are so readily subject to the temptation to proclaim Jesus as Lord when what we really mean is that we, his servants, are rulers of this or that province in his kingdom. We easily create little spheres of influence, of power, and we enjoy exercising it. We talk about the **kingdom of God** in the hope that some of that kingly glory will rub off on us. We draw attention to the promises about God's people in **Christ** being 'kings and **priests**' in order that we can lord it over others. And we quietly forget about the servant bits, the nuisance bits, the things which . . . yes, the things which Jesus would have done.

Of course, there are endless possibilities for self-deception here. We can so easily use the doing of menial tasks themselves as a way of avoiding the real and important, but demanding, vocations that we alone can fulfil. Or we can even use them as a way of showing how humble we are, so that we can be proud – of being humble! At that point the right answer is to laugh at ourselves and get on with something else.

The point is that, for us as for Jesus, we should be looking away from ourselves, and *at* the world we are supposed to be serving. Where the world's needs and our vocation meet is where we ought to be, ready to take on insignificant roles if that's what God wants, or to be publicly visible if that is our calling. And, as with Jesus, the picture of footwashing is meant to serve not only as a picture of all sorts of menial tasks that we may be called to perform, without drawing attention to them. It also points towards the much larger challenge, the challenge that Jesus issued to Peter in the last chapter of the book, the challenge to follow Jesus all the way to the cross, to lay down **life** itself in the service of God and the world he came to save.

Balancing the warning about servants not being greater than their master is the promise at the end of the passage. Those who go in Jesus' name, who get on with whatever work he gives them to do in his **spirit** and his love, are given an extraordinary status and privilege. Anyone who welcomes them, welcomes Jesus, and thereby also welcomes 'the one who sent him'. You probably won't realize it at the time. You'll be too busy thinking of the people you're working for and with. But, as you look back, you may be startled by the joy of realizing that as you walked into that house, that hospital, that place of pain or love or sorrow or hope, Jesus was walking in, wearing your skin, speaking in your tone of voice. 'I've given you a pattern,' he said, and he meant it.

JOHN 13.21–30

Judas Goes Out

²¹After saying this, Jesus was troubled in his spirit. He told them why.

'I'm telling you the solemn truth,' he said. 'One of you will betray me.'

²²The disciples looked at each other in shock, wondering who he could be talking about. ²³One of the disciples, the one Jesus specially loved, was reclining at table close beside him. ²⁴Simon Peter motioned to him to ask who it was he was talking about. ²⁵So, leaning as he was very close beside Jesus, he asked him, 'Who is it, master?'

²⁶'It's the one I'm going to give this piece of bread to', said Jesus, 'when I've dipped it in the dish.'

So he dipped the piece of bread, and gave it to Judas, son of Simon Iscariot. ²⁷After the bread, the satan entered into him.

'Do it quickly, won't you?' said Jesus to him.

²⁸None of the others at the table knew what he meant. ²⁹Because Judas kept the common purse, some were thinking that he meant, 'Buy what we need for the festival', or that he was to give something to the poor.

³⁰So when Judas had taken the bread, he went out at once. It was night.

A priest working in the villages outside Cambridge reports that when sheep are taken off to be killed, they know instinctively that the slaughterhouse is a bad place. They can smell or sense something which warns of danger. The lorry carrying them will stop, the gangplank will be put down, but they will refuse to move.

The slaughterhouse operators have devised a way of getting round the problem. They keep a sheep on the premises, who is used to the place and doesn't mind it any more. They take it up the plank on to the lorry, and then it walks down again quite happily. The other sheep, seeing one of their own leading the way, will follow.

The slaughterhouse workers call this sheep 'Judas'.

The present passage places side by side the two **disciples** who, in this **gospel**, are at the opposite extremes. Here we have 'the beloved disciple', the one who many still think was John himself, the writer of the gospel. The picture we get is of a young lad, perhaps the youngest of them all. If he was indeed John the son of Zebedee, he may have been a cousin of Jesus on his mother's side. He may not yet have been twenty. He had looked up at Jesus all his life, had followed him with joy and devotion (if not always, yet, with total understanding). Jesus had, as we say, a special affection for him, a soft spot. The others didn't resent it, perhaps because he was, after all, only a lad. They didn't find him a threat.

So close was their relationship that he was able to ask Jesus the question the others all wanted to put. People celebrating the Passover reclined on couches as a symbol of freedom (free people reclined to eat; slaves sat or stood). The beloved disciple was reclining close beside Jesus. He could whisper to him, and hear what was whispered back. It is one of the great pictures of friendship in all literature. And it is side by side with one of the greatest pictures of friendship betrayed.

When, so soon after that marvellous moment of the foot-washing, Jesus came out with the shocking statement that one of them was going to betray him, nobody had any idea who he was talking about. The medieval paintings of the Last Supper get it wrong: they tend to show Judas as a very obvious traitor, with his clothes, his face, his money-bag and his body language all telling us that he's the one. But the eleven others around the table didn't know. Judas was simply one of them.

Jesus had washed his feet, too. That in itself is worth pondering deeply. Even when Jesus spoke cryptically to him, and he went out, the others didn't understand what was happening.

They thought he was running an ordinary errand. (We should note that 'giving something to the poor' was not a special event; it was taken for granted, the sort of thing that people with enough to live on, albeit not by much, did all the time.)

Dipping a piece of bread in the dish and passing it to someone was a sign of special friendship. That was the sign Jesus employed to tell the beloved disciple not only that it was Judas who was going to do the awful deed, but what the deepest dimension of that deed would be. It was a betrayal of intimate, close trust and friendship. John has already told us that the **devil** had put the idea into Judas' mind to betray Jesus. Now he tells us that when Jesus gave Judas the bread, '**the satan**' entered into him.

John does not, I think, mean that Judas became 'demon-possessed' in the same way as those unfortunate characters we meet from time to time in the other gospels. The word 'satan' in Hebrew means 'accuser'; it's a legal term for someone who brings a prosecution, a charge, against someone else. What we are now to witness is Judas being used by the forces of darkness to bring a charge against Jesus, the messenger of the light. The confrontation between light and darkness, which has been hanging over the gospel story ever since the Prologue (1.5), is coming to its climax. And Judas has been willingly enlisted among the forces of darkness. The end of verse 30 is one of John's master-touches as a storyteller. The door opens on to the dark night, in every sense and at every level, and Judas disappears into it.

In the middle of the picture we have Jesus, flanked by love and betrayal. Perhaps it is always like this. Perhaps they always go together in this life, the joy and the agony, the intimacy and the knife in the back. Maybe Jesus' openness to the one meant that he was bound to be open to the other as well. Maybe it is like that for us too.

If and when it is, there is strange comfort to be had in Jesus' words to Judas. 'Do it quickly,' he said. He knew the agony that awaited him, and he didn't want it to go on any longer than it had to. As in 12.27, so here in 13.21, Jesus is troubled in **spirit**. There is no shame in spirit-trouble; it's what you get when you're a footwasher, a generous-love person, open to deep friendship and to the serious wounds that only friends can give. But John, in describing the entry of 'the satan' into Judas, knows that even the satanic purpose is held firmly within the overarching purposes of love, of liberation. The light will go on shining in the darkness, and the darkness will not master it.

JOHN 13.31–38

Love One Another

³¹When Judas had gone out, Jesus began to speak.

'Now the son of man is glorified!' he said. 'Now God is glorified in him! ³²And if God is glorified in him, God will glorify him in himself, and glorify him at once. ³³Children, I'm only with you a little longer. You will look for me, and, as I said to the Judaeans that where I was going they couldn't come, so I'm saying the same to you now.

³⁴'I'm giving you a new commandment, and it's this: love one another! Just as I have loved you, so you must love one another. ³⁵This is how everybody will know that you are my disciples, if you have love for each other.'

³⁶Simon Peter spoke up.

'Master,' he said, 'where are you going?'

'Where I'm going', replied Jesus, 'you can't follow me just now. You will follow later, though.'

³⁷'Master,' Peter replied, 'why can't I follow you now? I will lay down my life for you!'

³⁸'Will you really lay down your life for me?' smiled Jesus. 'I'm telling you the solemn truth: by the time the cock crows you will have disowned me three times.'

The question from the Greeks at the feast told Jesus that his time had come (12.23). In the same way, the disappearance of Judas, going out into the night, tells Jesus that his time, his great moment, is rushing upon him like a tidal wave. As the door shuts, a sense of excitement grips the narrative. It is as though Jesus is drawing the eleven closer to himself, telling them new things, things he couldn't say when Judas was there, things he must now say quickly precisely because Judas has gone and the time is very short.

This is where the 'farewell discourses', as they are often called, really start. The **disciples** ask questions from time to time, but from now until the end of chapter 16 Jesus is explaining to them the fact that he is 'going away', and that they can't follow him just yet. He is showing them what it all means for their future life, their own sorrow and joy and mission in the world. This then ends with the great prayer of chapter 17, after which the story picks up again with the arrest in the garden.

These chapters have often rightly been seen as among the most precious and intimate in the New Testament. They are full of comfort, challenge and hope, full of the deep and strange personal relationship that Jesus longs to have with each of his followers. We shouldn't be surprised that they are also full of some of the richest theological insights, of a sense of discovering who the true God is, and what he's doing in the world and in us. Where you find true devotion, you often find rich theology, and vice versa. Shallow thinking and shallow loving often keep company.

This is only the second time that Jesus has spoken of the **son of man** being 'glorified' (the other is 12.23). Before this moment (chapters 12 and 13 really go together in this respect), he has spoken of *God* being glorified, and of the 'son of man' being 'lifted up'. Now he puts the two together. As in Daniel 7, 'one like a son of man' will be exalted, coming on the clouds

54

to the Ancient of Days, and the whole scene will be the moment of God's glory, revealing who the true God is, over against the dark forces of the world that have resisted him and trampled upon his worshippers. You can feel the excitement in verses 31–32: glory, glory, glory, glory! Jesus is overwhelmed with glory, with the coming events as the unveiling of God's glory, with his own vocation rushing towards its conclusion and bringing God glory.

He is also overwhelmed by the fact that he is going to leave the disciples behind. He has only been with them a short while, and now he must go. Few teachers would be able to face such a moment without qualms. The disciples have learnt so little, understood so little, grasped so little of what their wonderful master has been doing in their midst. How will they cope without him?

The next three chapters will provide the answer, as Jesus makes the disciples solemn promises about the coming **holy spirit** who will continue to guide them as he himself had done. But before he even gets to that, he has something else to offer them: the simplest, clearest and hardest command of all. Love one another.

He describes it as a 'new commandment'. Love, of course, is central in many parts of the Old Testament. The book Leviticus (19.18) commanded the Israelites to love their neighbours as themselves. But the newness isn't so much a matter of never having heard words like this before. It's a matter of the mode of this love, the depth and type of this love: love one another *in the same way that I have loved you.*

It has been hard for the disciples up to this point even to appreciate what Jesus has been doing on their behalf; now he's telling them to copy him! As with the footwashing, they are to look back at his whole life, his whole way and manner of life, and to find in it a pattern, a shape, an example, a power. To wash someone else's feet, you have to think of yourself as only a slave. That, as we saw, can feed all the wrong kind of thinking: it can produce a sort of inverted pride, a pride at one's own humility. But with love there's no danger of that. Love is all about the other person. It overflows into service, not in order to show off how hard-working it is, but because that is its natural form.

This is to be the badge that the Christian community wears before the watching world. As we read verse 35 we are bound to cringe with shame at the way in which professing Christians have treated each other down the years. We have turned the **gospel** into a weapon of our own various cultures. We have hit each other over the head with it, burnt each other at the stake with it. We have defined the 'one another' so tightly that it means only 'love the people who reinforce your own sense of who you are'.

Like a child returning to the question it wanted to ask after the conversation has moved on elsewhere, Peter harks back to what Jesus said in verse 33, even though verses 34 and 35 contain some of the most beautiful and challenging words ever spoken. Once again he and Jesus banter to and fro, with Peter blustering away and saying whatever comes into his head. This time, though, the conversation suddenly runs into a brick wall. Peter doesn't realize what he's said. 'Where are you going? I'll follow you! I *want* to follow you! I'll lay down my life for you . . .'

'Will you really, Peter?' replies Jesus, and we can see the soft, sad smile as he says it. 'Is it really *you* that's going to lay down *your* life for *me*? Have you forgotten what I said about the shepherd and the sheep? Actually, Peter, I hate to say it, but what *you* are about to do is something rather different . . .'

We love Peter because he is so like the rest of us. And we love Jesus because he is so gentle with him, so loving, even within the sadness and the challenge and the glory that is to come. And once again we pause and reflect on how, in the strange purposes of God, love and betrayal, glory and denial, go so closely together.

JOHN 14.1–11

The Way, the Truth, the Life

[1]'Don't let your hearts be troubled,' Jesus continued. 'Trust God – and trust me, too! [2]There is plenty of room to live in my father's house. If that wasn't the case, I'd have told you, wouldn't I? I'm going to get a place ready for you! [3]And if I do go and get a place ready for you, I will come back and take you to be with me, so that you can be there, where I am. [4]You know the way where I'm going, after all.'

[5]'Actually, master,' said Thomas to him, 'we don't know where you're going, so how can we know the way?'

[6]'I am the way,' replied Jesus, 'and the truth and the life! Nobody comes to the father except through me. [7]If you had known me, you would have known my father. From now on you do know him! You have seen him!'

[8]'Just show us the father, then, master,' said Philip to Jesus, 'and that'll be good enough for us!'

[9]'Have I been with you for such a long time, Philip,' replied Jesus, 'and still you don't know me? Anyone who has seen me has seen the father! How can you say, "Show us the father"? [10]Don't you believe that I am in the father, and the father is in me? The words I'm speaking to you, I'm not speaking on my own initiative. It's the father, who lives within me, who is doing his own works. [11]You must trust me that I am in the father and the father is in me. If not, then trust because of all the things you've seen done.'

'Are you sure there'll be room for us all?'

We were on our way back to a friend's house. There were two carloads of us, relaxed and happy after a football match which we'd won. The match had been at another school several miles away, and rather than going back to our own school, and from there to our homes, we'd arranged that we would stay with one member of the team who lived much closer to where the game had been played.

'I told you, didn't I?' he said. 'You'll see. There's plenty of room for you all.'

We had been imagining he lived in an ordinary house on an ordinary street. Even with an extension built on the back, as some of our friends had, ordinary houses only had four bedrooms, or five at the most. How could he manage to squeeze in ten of us? Were we all going to sleep on the living-room floor? What would his parents say?

We turned into the driveway, and then we realized. This wasn't an ordinary street, and it wasn't an ordinary house. It was a mansion. He grinned, a bit shyly.

'Told you there would be room, didn't I?'

We tumbled out and he took us upstairs. Long corridors, lots of rooms. We couldn't believe it. It was like a hotel. His father's house.

That's the image Jesus is using. He is going away, and the **disciples** are naturally anxious about where he's going and whether they will be able to follow him. So he speaks of 'his father's house'. The only other time he's used the expression it referred to the **Temple** (2.16). The point about the Temple, within the life of the people of Israel, was that it was the place where **heaven** and earth met. Now Jesus hints at a new city, a new world, a new 'house'. Heaven and earth will meet again when God renews the whole world. At that time there will be room for everyone.

This promise is made as a way of assuring the disciples that, though he's going away, it will be for their benefit; he won't forget them, he won't abandon them. But it reaches out, beyond the disciples on that dark spring evening, and embraces all of us. These words are often used at funerals, and we can understand why. We can't see the way ahead, and we need to know not only that there is indeed a way into the unknown future, but that we will be able to find it.

Thomas, in character, is grumpy. 'What d'you mean, we know the way? We don't éven know where you're going!'

Jesus' reply has haunted and confronted the world's imagination ever since. 'I am the way.' If you want to know how to get to the father's house, you must come with me.

Within the Western world of the last two centuries or so, this saying of Jesus has become one of the most controversial. 'I am the way and the truth and the life!' How dare he, people have asked. How dare John, or the church, or anyone else, put such words into anyone's mouth? Isn't this the height of arrogance, to imagine that Jesus or anyone else was the *only* way? Don't we now know that this attitude has done untold damage around the world, as Jesus' followers have insisted that everyone else should give up their own ways of life and follow his instead? I know people, professing Christians, for whom it seems that their central article of **faith** is their rejection of this idea of Jesus' uniqueness.

The trouble with this is that it doesn't work. If you dethrone Jesus, you enthrone something, or someone, else instead. The belief that 'all religions are really the same' sounds nice and democratic – though the study of religions quickly shows that it isn't true. What you are really saying if you claim that they're all the same is that none of them are more than distant echoes, distorted images, of reality. You're saying that 'reality', God, 'the divine', is remote and unknowable, and that neither Jesus nor Buddha nor Moses nor Krishna gives us direct access to it. They all provide *a* way towards the foothills of the mountain, not *the* way to the summit.

It isn't just John's **gospel** that you lose if you embrace this idea. The whole New Testament – the whole of early Christianity – insists that the one true and living God, the creator, is the God of Israel; and that the God of Israel has acted decisively, within history, to bring Israel's story to its proper goal, and through that to address, and rescue, the world. The idea of a vague general truth, to which all 'religions' bear some kind of oblique witness, is foreign to Christianity. It is, in fact, in its present form, part of the eighteenth-century protest *against* Christianity – even though some people produce it like a rabbit out of a hat, as though it was quite a new idea.

The real answer is that, though of course it's true that many Christians and churches have been arrogant in the way they have presented the gospel, the whole setting of this passage shows that such arrogance is a denial of the very truth it's claiming to present. The truth, the life, through which we know and find the way, is Jesus himself: the Jesus who washed the disciples' feet and told them to copy his example, the Jesus who was on his way to give his life as the shepherd for the sheep. Was that arrogant? Was that self-serving? Only when the church recovers the nerve to follow Jesus in his own mission and vocation, I suspect, will it be able to recover its nerve fully in making the claim of verse 6.

Unless it does, though, it loses also the vision of the father which this whole passage sets out before us. Don't come with a set, fixed idea of who God is, and try to fit Jesus into that. Look at Jesus, the Jesus who wept at the tomb of his friend, the Jesus who washed his followers' feet, and you'll see who is the true God. That was Jesus' answer to Philip. It is his answer to the natural questions that arise in people's minds today. Only when his followers are themselves continuing to do what Jesus did may they be believed when they speak the earth-shattering truth that he spoke.

JOHN 14.12–21

Another Helper

[12]'I'm telling you the solemn truth,' Jesus continued. 'Anyone who trusts in me will also do the works that I'm doing. In fact, they will do greater works than these, because I'm going to the father! [13]And whatever you ask in my name, I will do it, so that the father may be glorified in the son. [14]If you ask anything in my name, I will do it.

[15]'If you love me,' he went on, 'you will keep my commands. [16]And I will ask the father, and he will give you another helper, to be with you for ever. [17]This other helper is the spirit of truth. The world can't receive him, because it doesn't see him or know him. But you know him, because he lives with you, and will be in you.

[18]'I'm not going to leave you bereft. I am coming to you. [19]Not long from now, the world won't see me any more; but you will see me. Because I live, you will live too. [20]On that day you will know that I am in my father, and you in me, and I in you.

[21]'Anyone who has my commandments and keeps them – that's the person who loves me. Anyone who loves me will be loved by my father, and I will love them and show myself to them.'

'If only we'd been there when Jesus was around!' people often say. 'It would have been so much easier. He would have explained everything to us, and told us what to do. And he'd have been such an encouragement. Whatever we were doing, he'd be positive about it, and we'd want to go on and do even better.'

It's a common perception, but it's wrong on two counts.

First, the evidence of the four **gospels** suggests that the people who were around in Jesus' day didn't see it like that themselves. Some of his closest friends betrayed and denied him. Even the beloved **disciple** ran away in the garden. Most

61

people couldn't really make him out. He was compelling but puzzling. Many thought he was mad.

Second, in this passage and several others in the next two chapters, we find that Jesus *has* promised to be 'around' with his people from that day to this. In fact, he's promised that it will be easier, not harder, in this new mode. His people will be able to do things they couldn't do when he was physically present.

But how will he be 'around', now?

He has promised to send us his own **spirit**, his own breath, his own inner life. Here, and for the next two chapters, he uses a special word to describe the spirit. In verse 16 he says that the father will give us 'another helper'. This 'helper' is the spirit.

But the word I've translated 'helper' is rich and many-sided. It doesn't simply mean someone who comes to lend assistance in our various tasks. It certainly does mean that as well: the spirit, as we'll be seeing, comes to give God's people the strength and energy to do what they have to do, to live for God and witness to his love in the world. But it means two other things as well.

One word sometimes used is 'comforter'. Comfort is a strange and wonderful thing. Have you noticed how, when someone is deeply distressed, after a bereavement or a tragedy, the fact of having other people with them, hugging them and being alongside them, gives them strength for the next moment, then the one after that, then the one after that? Outwardly nothing has changed. The tragedy is still a tragedy. The dead person won't be coming back. But other human support changes our ability to cope with disaster. It gives us strength. When the spirit is spoken of as the 'comforter', this kind of extra strength to meet special need is in mind.

But there is something quite different as well. An equally good translation for the word is 'advocate'. An advocate stands up in a court of law and explains to the judge or jury how things are from his or her client's point of view. The advocate pleads the case. Jesus assumes that his followers will often find themselves, as he found himself, on the wrong side of official persecution. He saw the situation, as centuries of Jewish tradition had done before him, in terms of the heavenly lawcourt with God as the judge. In that court, his people can rest assured that their case will be heard, that God will constantly be reminded of their plight, because the spirit will plead on their behalf. (Paul says much the same in Romans 8.26–27.)

As a result of this promised spirit, the spirit of Jesus himself, Christians now, remarkable though it may seem, are in a better situation even than the followers of Jesus during his lifetime. They were sometimes able to do remarkable things even then; Jesus gave them the power, in the other gospel accounts, to perform healings like his own (e.g. Luke 9.1–6; 10.17). But mostly they were following him in some perplexity, and when he wasn't there they couldn't do very much (e.g. Mark 8.18, 28–29).

But now, by the spirit, they will be able to do all kinds of things. When Jesus 'goes to the father' – in other words, when he defeats the power of death through his own death and **resurrection** – then all sorts of new possibilities will be opened in front of them. The 'works' he has been doing, as he says again and again, are the evidence that the father is at work in him. Now he says that the disciples will do even greater works than these!

It's in that setting, too, that he makes the first of several remarkable promises about prayer. 'Whatever you ask in my name, I will do it.' The all-important phrase 'in my name' doesn't, of course, just mean adding 'in the name of Jesus' to anything we might think of, however stupid, selfish or hurtful. The 'name', after all, as in many cultures, is supposed to reveal the character. Yesterday I looked out of the window and saw some demonstrators protesting against something the government was doing. 'Not in my name!' their posters said. What they meant was: 'You are claiming to represent this country, but I am dissociating myself from what you're doing! You're not doing it in my name!'

Praying 'in Jesus' name', then, means that, as we get to know who Jesus is, so we find ourselves drawn into his life and love and sense of purpose. We will then begin to see what needs doing, what we should be aiming at within our sphere of possibilities, and what resources we need to do it. When we then ask, it will be 'in Jesus' name', and to his glory; and, through that, to the glory of the father himself (verse 13). But, when all this is understood, we shouldn't go soft on that marvellous word *anything*. He said it, and he means it.

The last three verses of this section present a wonderful circle of promises that are ours because of Jesus' being with us by the spirit. We will 'see' him, plain to the eye of **faith**. We will live with his new life. We will know the deepest theological knowledge of all: that he and the father are 'in' each other, and that we are 'in' him and he 'in' us. And we will be joined to Jesus and the father by an unbreakable bond of love. This, in turn, leads back where the sequence began. He will show himself to us. All the main themes of the gospel so far are now revealed for what they are: truths about the inner life of the father and son, truths which turn to fire and love and invite us to warm ourselves within their inmost circle.

JOHN 14.22–31

My Peace I Give to You

²²Judas spoke up. (This was the other Judas, not Iscariot.)

'Master,' he said, 'how will it be that you will show yourself to us and not to the world?'

²³'If anyone loves me,' Jesus replied, 'they will keep my word. My father will love them, and we will come to them and make

our home with them. [24]Anyone who doesn't love me won't keep my word. And the word which you hear isn't mine. It comes from the father, who sent me.

[25]'I've said all this to you while I'm here with you. [26]But the helper, the holy spirit, the one the father will send in my name, he will teach you everything. He will bring back to your mind everything I've said to you.

[27]'I'm leaving you peace. I'm giving you my own peace. It's quite different from what the world gives. Don't let your hearts be troubled; don't be fearful. [28]You heard that I said to you, "I'm going away, and I'm coming back to you." If you loved me, you would be glad, because I'm going to the father – because the father is greater than me. [29]And now I've told you before it happens, so that when it does happen, you may believe.

[30]'I haven't got much more to say to you. The ruler of this world is coming. He has nothing to do with me. [31]But all this is happening so that the world may know that I love the father, and that I'm doing what the father has told me to do.

'Get up. Let's be going.'

'I'm going to tell the whole world about it!'

She had just got engaged. This was the moment she'd dreamed about. The happiest day of her life. She wanted everyone to know.

But what did she mean by 'the world'?

We found out quite quickly. It meant, basically, working through her list of telephone numbers and having a breathless, excited call with each of the people on it. That must have been about thirty people, each with their familes, say three more each: 120 people, a small drop in the large ocean called 'the world'. Then there was the announcement in the newspaper, which must have been seen by ten thousand or so; a significant step up from 120, but still not that many. But that was as far as it went. That was 'the world', for better or for worse.

Or think what people mean when they say, 'Be quiet! I don't want the whole world to know about it!' If something has happened which is embarrassing or shaming, people are afraid that gossip will carry the news far and wide. They begin to suspect that strangers in the street are talking about them behind their back. Here 'the world' means something threatening: a large, shapeless but dangerous mass of people 'out there'. Most cultures and societies, and certainly most individuals and families, find themselves thinking of 'us' and 'the world', sometimes in friendly alliance, sometimes in suspicion or confrontation.

When Jesus, in John's **gospel**, speaks of 'the world', it is more in the second sense. Think back to the Prologue (1.10): he was in the world, the world was made by him, but the world didn't know him. What is 'the world' here? It is the whole created order; but it's also the people who inhabit it, and who have rebelled against their creator. Jesus has, however, come 'into the world' (1.9), because 'God loved the world so much' (3.16) that he sent his son 'to rescue the world'.

Confused? You might well be. But the confusion isn't John's fault. It comes from the way in which human wickedness has distorted everything. God's proper answer to this is *both* that he rejects wickedness and remains totally opposed to it, *and* that he loves the world, and the people, that he made, despite that wickedness. Jesus' coming into the world, as we have seen all along, brings both of these divine answers onto the stage of human history. He comes as the light of the world, so that people can have the light of **life**; but many prefer the darkness.

Because of all this, the farewell discourses of chapters 14, 15 and 16 say a lot about 'the world' as the place of danger and darkness, the place where the **disciples** will find themselves after Jesus has gone. They will know him, but 'the world' will not (verse 22), because they will love him and keep his **word** (helped by the **holy spirit** bringing things back to their memories). 'The world', by contrast, will do neither of these (verse 23). There is no attempt here to make the kind of compromise that many Christians settle for, bending over backwards to discover places where they and 'the world' are not so far apart after all. That is often the right thing to do; but the fact remains that much of 'the world', to this day, does not love Jesus and does not keep his word. To pretend otherwise, with all the horrors of both ancient and modern times, would be madness.

There is, then, a sharp distinction between the followers of Jesus and 'the world'. Only when that is recognized can the next word be heard, which is another spectacular promise. Those who hold fast to Jesus, and refuse to settle for a second-best, compromised discipleship, will find that his peace comes to them as a gift, a peace of a kind that 'the world' can never give (verse 27). This peace will assure them of his presence and support, gladdening them with the knowledge that the Jesus they know and love is indeed one with the father.

The way to this peace, however, is through the sharp conflict that is about to come. 'The ruler of this world' is on his way, even now, coming to arrest Jesus.

Who is this 'ruler'?

At one level, it is Caesar, whose soldiers will take Jesus to his death not many hours hence. At another level, it is the dark power that stands behind even Caesar, the spiritual force of wickedness named so briefly in the previous chapter, now using Judas as a poor, willing accomplice. The phrase 'the world' gets its negative force in John's gospel from the fact that the present world, though loved and claimed by the father, remains under the rule of this dark lord. Jesus' approaching death and **resurrection** will inflict a huge wound on this rule, from which it will never recover; but the disciples are to be sent out into the world where opposition is still powerful and deadly.

Their courage and confidence is to be sustained by remembering what Jesus had done. He did what he did so that 'the world' might know that he loved the father. Called to follow him, we are to act in such a way that 'the world' will know that we love him.

The strange little command at the end of the passage seems to indicate that at this point Jesus led the disciples out of the room where they'd had the meal, and off to the garden of Gethsemane. If that's correct, then the next chapters might be imagined as being spoken as they walked through the darkened streets of the city; but perhaps we shouldn't press John too much for this sort of detail. Enough that we 'hear' this passage as we continue our own walk through the dark streets of 'the world', following the one true light.

JOHN 15.1–8

The True Vine

[1]'I am the true vine', said Jesus, 'and my father is the gardener. [2]He cuts off every branch of mine that doesn't bear fruit; and he prunes every branch that does bear fruit, so that it can bear more fruit. [3]You are already clean. That's because of the word that I've spoken to you.

[4]'Remain in me, and I will remain in you! The branch can't bear fruit by itself, but only if it remains in the vine. In the same way, you can't bear fruit unless you remain in me. [5]I am the vine, you are the branches. People who remain in me, and I in them, are the ones who bear plenty of fruit. Without me, you see, you can't do anything.

[6]'If people don't remain in me, they are thrown out, like a branch, and they wither. People collect the branches and put them on the fire, and they are burned. [7]If you remain in me, and my words remain in you, ask for whatever you want, and it will happen for you. [8]My father is glorified in this: that you bear plenty of fruit, and so become my disciples.'

One of many areas in which I possess near-total incompetence is gardening. We have moved house so many times that I have never had the chance to develop an instinct for which plants do well where and in what kind of soil and light. Once or twice I have picked up books on how to do it, but usually I haven't got beyond the first couple of pages. Like some theology books, the opening pages of gardening books, and cookery books if it comes to that, often have three long words I don't understand; or, worse, three ordinary words which they're obviously using in a special sense unknown to me.

I am no gardener, then. But I can mow a lawn. I can pick gooseberries. I can plant bulbs (on the 'dig-a-hole-and-drop-them-in' principle).

And I can prune roses. Someone told me how when I was young and I've never forgotten. In fact, I not only know *how* to do it, I even know *why* (well, more or less). A rose bush, left to itself, will get straggly and tangled, and grow in on itself. It will produce quite a lot of not-so-good roses rather than a smaller number of splendid ones. It will, quite literally, get in its own light. It needs help to grow in the right directions and to the right ends. So you prune it to stop it wasting its energy and being unproductive. You cut out, particularly, the parts of the plant that are growing inwards and getting tangled up. You encourage the shoots that are growing outwards, toward the light. You prune the rose, in other words, to help it to be its true self.

As far as I understand it, more or less the same thing works with vines. (We were once given a vine, but we moved house before pruning-time came around. The last I heard, it had grown right out of the greenhouse door, which can't have done the vine, or the greenhouse, much good.) Vines, too, need to focus their energy on producing good quality grapes, rather than lots of second-rate ones. Vines, too, need to grow towards the light rather than getting in a tangled mass. Left to themselves, they produce a lot of superfluous growth which must be cut away if the vine is truly to be what it's capable of.

The English language doesn't let us catch the flavour of what John writes here. The word he uses for 'prune' in verse 2 is unusual, and is very like the word for 'clean' or 'pure' in the next verse. That is why he's used it here: he wants us to link the 'pruning' of the vine with the 'clean' state of the **disciples**. They have already been 'pruned', though no doubt there is more of it to come. Jesus has spoken the **word** to them, calling them to take up their cross and follow him. They have had to submit to the pruner's knife, cutting away other goals and ambitions. They have already borne fruit; they must now expect more pruning, so that they can bear more fruit.

Within Jewish tradition, the vine was a picture of Israel. God brought a vine out of Egypt, and planted it in the promised land (Psalm 80.8–18). It had been ravaged by wild animals and needed protecting and re-establishing. The vineyard of Israel, said Isaiah in chapter 5, has borne wild grapes instead of proper ones. Other prophets used the same picture.

Now Jesus is saying that *he* is the 'true vine'. This can only mean that he is, in himself, the true Israel. He is the one on whom God's purposes are now resting. And his followers are members of God's true people – if they belong to him and remain 'in' him. The picture of the 'vine' isn't just a clever illustration from gardening. It is about who Jesus and his people really are, and what is now going to happen to them as a result.

Within the farewell discourses as a whole, this section opens up a whole new dimension of what Jesus wants to say as he takes his leave of his closest associates. He has already spoken of them being 'in him', as he is 'in the father' (14.20). Now we see more of what this means. On the one hand, it is a way of speaking of himself as Israel-in-person, and of his followers as members of God's true people because they belong to him. On the other hand, it is a way of speaking of the intimate relationship with him that they are to enjoy, and (so to speak) to cultivate. Branches that decide to 'go it alone', to try living without the life of the vine, soon discover their mistake. They wither and die, and are good for nothing but the fire (verse 6). But branches that remain in the vine, and submit to the pruner's knife when necessary, live and bear fruit. That is the prospect that Jesus holds out to his followers, to all of us.

The urgent question, then, is this. How do we 'remain' in him? What does it look like in practice? Both of the meanings above come into play. We must remain in the community that knows and loves him and celebrates him as its Lord. There is no such thing as a solitary Christian. We can't 'go it alone'. But we must also remain as people of prayer and worship in our own intimate, private lives. We must make sure to be in touch, in tune, with Jesus, knowing him and being known by him. Once again, the most extraordinary promises about prayer (verse 7) accompany the sharpest warnings (verse 6).

And, though it always hurts, we must be ready for the father's pruning knife. God is glorified, and so will we be, by bearing good quality fruit, and lots of it. For that to happen, there will be extra growth that needs cutting away. That, too, is an intimate process. The vine-dresser is never closer to the vine, taking more thought over its long-term health and productivity, than when he has the knife in his hand.

JOHN 15.9–17

Obeying and Loving

9'As the father loved me,' Jesus continued, 'so I loved you. Remain in my love. 10If you keep my commands, you will remain in my love, just as I have kept my father's commands, and remain in his love. 11I've said these things to you so that my joy may be in you, and so that your joy may be full.

> ¹²'This is my command: love one another, in the same way that I loved you. ¹³No one has a love greater than this, to lay down your life for your friends. ¹⁴You are my friends, if you do what I tell you. ¹⁵I'm not calling you "servants" any longer; servants don't know what their master is doing. But I've called you "friends", because I've let you know everything I heard from my father.
>
> ¹⁶'You didn't choose me. I chose you, and I appointed you to go and bear fruit, fruit that would last. Then the father will give you whatever you ask in my name. ¹⁷This is my command to you: love one another.'

Like an innocent child wandering by itself into a kitchen and pressing the switches that will set the house on fire, some biblical texts have been taken out of their original setting and used in ways that would have horrified the original speaker or writer. Here in this passage we have one with exactly that history.

'No one', said Jesus, 'has a love greater than this, to lay down your life for your friends' (verse 13). That is true, gloriously true. Indeed, Jesus was on his way to his own execution as the most dramatic example of the point (see 10.11; 13.1). The cross is clearly in view here, when Jesus says that laying down your life for your friends is the highest form of love, and then says 'and you, of course, are my friends' (verse 14). But during the First World War (1914–18), this text was used again and again, in sermons and lectures, set to music and sung by great choirs, with one single meaning: therefore *you*, young man – they were mostly young men – must go off to the front line, do what you're told and if necessary die for your country.

They did, in their tens of thousands. God honours, I believe, the self-sacrifice and dedication of those who sincerely and devoutly believed they were doing their duty. But I also believe God judges those who use texts like this as a convenient rhetorical trick to put moral pressure on other people, when what they needed was a bit of moral pressure on themselves to ask: Why are we doing this at all? If we must have a war, is this really the best way of fighting it? Are these '**sacrifices**' (another convenient 'religious' word; people spoke of 'the final sacrifice', forgetting that in the Bible human sacrifice was condemned over and over again) the best way both of winning the war and of preparing ourselves for the world that will need rebuilding after it's all over?

The easy identification of 'our' side with God's side has been a major problem ever since Christianity became the official religion of the Roman state in the fourth century. Ironically, as Western Europe has become less and less Christian in terms of its practice, its leaders seem to have made this identification more and more, so that both sides in the major world wars of the twentieth century were staffed, as we have already noted, by Christian chaplains praying for victory.

This sits uneasily alongside a passage like this one, where the talk is of love, not war. In a world of danger and wickedness, it won't do for everyone to pretend there are no hard decisions to be made. But precisely one of the great dangers, and great wickednesses, of the world is the very common belief that fighting is a fine thing, that war is a useful way of settling disputes, and that, to put it crudely, might is right. One of the reasons human civilization has struggled to promote justice is the recognition that things aren't that easy. And justice, at its best, knows that it has only a negative function: to clear the decks and leave the world open for people to love one another.

You can't legislate for love; but God, through Jesus, can command you to love. Discovering the difference between what law cannot achieve and what God can and does achieve is one of the great arts of being human, and of being Christian. In the present passage we are brought in on the secret of it all.

The 'command' to love is given by one who has himself done everything that love can do. When a mother loves a child, she creates the context in which the child is free to love her in return. When a ruler really does love his or her subjects, and when this becomes clear by generous and warm-hearted actions, he or she creates a context in which the subjects can and will love them in return. The parody of this, seen with awesome clarity in George Orwell's book *Nineteen Eighty-Four*, is when the totalitarian ruler ('Big Brother'), who has done nothing but oppress and terrify his subjects, nevertheless orders them to love him. And the devastating climax, after the initially resisting subjects have been brainwashed, is that it works. At the end of the book, the hero is, in a sense, happy. 'He loved Big Brother.' And the reader knows that at this moment the hero has ceased to be truly human.

Jesus, though, issues the command that we are to love one another, and so to remain in his love, because he has acted out, and will act out, the greatest thing that love can do. He has come to make us more human, not less. He has come to give us freedom and joy (verse 11), not slavery and a semi-human stupor. He has come so that we can bear fruit that will last (verse 16), whether in terms of a single life changed because we loved somebody as Jesus loved us, or in terms of a single decision that we had to take, a single task we had to perform, through which, though we couldn't see it at the time, the world became a different place. Love makes both the lover and the beloved more truly human.

At the heart of it all is the humility that comes from knowing who's in charge. 'You didn't choose me; I chose you' (verse 16). I was once asked, on the radio, which religion I would choose if I could. I pointed out that the idea of 'choosing your religion' was a mistake in the first place. Religions are not items on the supermarket shelf that we can pick and choose – though many today try to run their lives that way.

Or, if they are, you'd have to say that following Jesus wasn't a 'religion'. It is a personal relationship of love and loyalty to the one who has loved us more than we can begin to imagine. And the test of that love and loyalty remains the simple, profound, dangerous and difficult command: love one another.

JOHN 15.18–27

If the World Hates You

[18]'If the world hates you,' Jesus went on, 'know that it hated me before it hated you. [19]If you were from the world, the world would be fond of its own. But the world hates you for this reason: that you're not from the world. No: I chose you out of the world.

[20]'Remember the word that I said to you: servants are not greater than their masters. If they persecuted me, they will persecute you too. If they kept my word, they will keep yours too. [21]But they will do all these things to you because of my name, because they don't know the one who sent me.

[22]'If I hadn't come and spoken to them, they wouldn't be guilty of sin. But now they have no excuse for their sin. [23](Anyone who hates me, hates my father as well!) [24]If I hadn't done, there in the middle of them, the works which nobody else did, they wouldn't be guilty of sin. But now they have seen me, and my father – and they've hated us both! [25]All this has happened, however, so that the word in their law might be fulfilled: "They hated me for no reason."

[26]'When the helper comes – the one I shall send you from the father, the spirit of truth who comes from the father – he will give evidence about me. [27]And you will give evidence as well, because you have been with me from the start.'

We are all amateur psychiatrists now. Our modern culture has learnt enough from the founders of modern psychology and psychiatry for people to toss bits and pieces of it into ordinary conversations, articles in popular newspapers and television chat-shows. We know about 'phobias'. We know about 'neuroses' – at least, we probably don't know exactly what they are, but we know that to call someone 'neurotic' means that they aren't thinking straight and are in danger of not acting straight either. We know about 'Freudian slips' – when someone accidentally mentions something they were worried about, but were intending to keep secret.

And we know about 'paranoia'. It's a state of mind in which you are convinced that something bad is going to happen to you, that people hate you and are out to get you. (The professionals also use the word for people who are deluded into thinking they are very important; but in street-level usage it normally means that you imagine hostile people all around.) And many ordinary, well-adjusted Christians might imagine that this passage, at the end of John 15, was bordering on the paranoid. The world is going to hate you, says Jesus. The world will persecute you. The world is guilty, and it hates me and my father as well as you! We can imagine someone saying, 'Look here, how paranoid can you get?'

Well, the problem with paranoia is that sometimes people *are* out to get you. Six days before I wrote this, gunmen burst into a church in Pakistan and killed eighteen people at the end of a worship service. A long letter in today's newspaper gives information about many other places in the world where Christians are routinely attacked, beaten, robbed, or at least discriminated against, with little hope of any redress. (I should add that the Pakistan police have already captured some of the murderers from the incident I mentioned, and declare that they will bring them to justice.)

The young church certainly faced persecution from the very beginning. We know that, of course, not least because of the evidence given by one of the leading persecutors – Saul of Tarsus, who became the **apostle** Paul. He attacked the church violently, and then spent the rest of his life being himself attacked, beaten, stoned and constantly threatened. The first three hundred years of church history were a story of on–off persecution, usually more on than off. Since then, there have been many times and places where professing Christians have faced, and still do face, enormous and frequently violent hostility.

Yes, we must add that Christians have often persecuted other peoples and faiths. It is scandalous but true. The idea that the **gospel** of Jesus and his love could be spread by any kind of violence would be a sort of sick joke if it weren't such a serious mistake. And of course countries, rulers and societies that claim to be Christian have often used the name of Jesus **Christ** as an excuse to wage war on people with whom they had a quarrel that was nothing to do with Christianity. The loser in all such situations has been the gospel itself.

But this doesn't take away from the fact that Jesus' warnings in this section are not paranoid, even if they may sound like that to a comfortable, armchair version of Christianity. The world will hate you (verses 18–19); it will persecute you, as it persecuted Jesus (verses 20–21); it is guilty, because it has seen and rejected Jesus and the father (verses 22–25). This is, as you might say, the way the world is.

And 'the world' in question, from Jesus' perspective, was not the pagan world, the world of Greek and Roman culture, Caesar's world. It was 'the world' in which he was born and lived: the world of Galilee and Jerusalem, of the Galileans and Judaeans. It was the world of Abraham's children, people who were studying the **law** of Moses. It was the world which thought of itself as God's people. This was the world that looked at Jesus, at what he was doing, that listened to what he was saying, and that said 'No, thank you'. This was the world that saw the blind man healed, and remained blind itself. This was the world that saw Lazarus raised to **life**, and decided it would be safer to kill him off properly because otherwise people might believe in Jesus.

So who was being paranoid? Was it Jesus?

Or was it, rather, 'the world' itself, which saw the prince of peace as a threat, the lord of love as someone to hate? Who is being paranoid today when Christians find their churches attacked even though they were living quiet and restrained lives, allowing the witness of their daily honesty and integrity, their love and gentleness, to speak for itself? Who is being paranoid, when Christians speak up within Western democracies on behalf of the millions in the Southern hemisphere who suffer debt and deprivation through the policies of the rich minority, and when such Christians are told to stop being disruptive and 'political'?

And yet we can see why it happens. It's a dangerous truth, which could encourage delusions of grandeur, but it's true none the less, that Christians, followers of Jesus Christ, are 'not from the world' (verse 19). Like Jesus' own **kingdom** (18.36), they are *for* the world – sent into it, as Jesus was, to bear witness to God's love and to bring about his victory – but they are not *from* the world. This isn't just another way of reshuffling the religious cards, or even the political ones, and dealing them out again so that we can play the same game as before and perhaps have a different winner this time. This is a different game altogether.

Those who follow Jesus will find themselves in a new situation, facing new dangers as well as opportunities. Fortunately, they are not there alone. The 'helper' (see 14.16), the **spirit** of truth, will come from the father, and live in them, telling them, and telling the world through them, who Jesus really was and is. They mustn't get lured into talking about themselves. That might well make them paranoid, and it would make their hearers either bored or angry. They must talk about him. The world won't like it, but it must be done.

JOHN 16.1–11
The Spirit and the World

[1]'I've said these things to you', Jesus went on, 'to stop you from being tripped up. [2]They will put you out of the synagogues. In fact, the time is coming when anyone who kills you will suppose that they are in that way offering worship to God. [3]They will do these things because they haven't known the father, or me. [4]But I have been talking to you about these things so that, when their time comes, you will remember that I told you about them.

'I didn't say these things to you from the start, because you were with me. [5]But now I'm going to the one who sent me. None of you asks me, "Where are you going?" [6]But because I've said these things to you, sorrow has filled your heart. [7]However, it's the truth that I'm telling you: it's better for you that I should go away. If I don't go away, you see, the helper won't come to you. But if I go away, I will send him to you.

[8]'When he comes, he will prove the world to be in the wrong on three counts: sin, justice and judgment. [9]In relation to sin – because they don't believe in me! [10]In relation to justice – because I'm going to the father, and you won't see me any more. [11]In relation to judgment – because the ruler of this world is judged.'

I once saw a film based on one of Charles Dickens's novels. The film was about poverty and the degrading effect it has on people. One of the most depressing scenes was in a lawyer's office, as the relatives of a man imprisoned for debt were desperately trying to bring a lawsuit to prove that he was owed a large sum of money, which should be paid and earn him his release. The lawyers didn't care. Their clerks didn't care. Nobody cared. The case, written out on a fine piece of parchment, was rolled up, tied with a ribbon and left to gather dust along with dozens, hundreds, of others. Suddenly you could feel it: the cold realization that there was nothing you could do.

Justice deferred is usually justice denied. And it was being deferred indefinitely.

This kind of situation explains what many people find puzzling in several of the psalms. Again and again the writers call out to God, asking that he would judge them (e.g. Psalms 17, 26 and 43). We have got used to the words 'judge' and 'judgment' being used in a bad sense, to mean 'condemn' and 'condemnation'. But to the ordinary worshipper in ancient Israel, things looked very different. The problem was that they couldn't get their case to come to court. If only someone in authority could see what had happened and make the obvious decision! But they wouldn't and they didn't. So the Psalmists prayed that God would act as judge and decide who was in the right.

There were many times during Israel's history when the nation as a whole found itself in the same situation. Big, powerful foreign nations invaded, attacked, and devastated cities, captured thousands of people, and took them away as slaves. Eventually the remaining people, living in the Jerusalem area, were taken away to Babylon. Even after they had returned, they were overrun and oppressed by one foreign power after another. And they developed a regular way of thinking about it all, based on their unshakeable belief that their God, the world's creator, was the God of justice.

They imagined themselves in a lawcourt. (In the Hebrew system, there was no 'director of public prosecutions', so every lawsuit was brought by someone against someone else. The judge's job was to decide between the two of them: to vindicate or uphold the one and to condemn the other one.) Israel was bringing a lawsuit against the foreign nations. What right had Babylon got – had Syria got – had Egypt or Rome or any-one else got – to oppress God's people? What had they done to deserve it?

Sometimes – and you can imagine how daring this was –

there were prophets who accepted this as the scenario, but declared that actually Israel *had* deserved it. Isaiah spoke of Israel rebelling against **YHWH** and YHWH being right to bring condemnation against the people. So did Jeremiah. So, in a memorable chapter, did Daniel (chapter 9).

But the prophets, including those same ones, regularly went on to see God taking his seat in judgment again, and this time bringing a different verdict. God would find in favour of Israel, and against the nations that had wickedly and arrogantly attacked it. This time, the lawsuit would go Israel's way. This time, God would demonstrate that the world was in the wrong and that his people were in the right.

Once you grasp that whole way of thinking, and the Jewish way of looking at the world which goes with it, you are ready to understand the otherwise very difficult passage which is the key moment in this section. Verses 8–11 speak of the **holy spirit**, the 'helper' we've already met in the previous chapters, coming as the advocate in a lawsuit, and *proving that the world is in the wrong*. The difference is that this time God's people in the lawsuit are the followers of Jesus. 'The world' includes of course the pagan nations, but also, insofar as it hasn't believed in Jesus, Israel as well.

The earlier verses of the section repeat what's been said before, adding new emphases. Persecution is on its way for those who follow Jesus. It will mean being put out of the synagogue (as with the man born blind, in chapter 9). It may well mean death (as with the frequent threats against Jesus, and also against Lazarus in 12.10). And now that Jesus is going away, his followers need to know how things will be. They are bound to be sad, but they should be comforted by the arrival of the 'helper', the holy spirit.

In particular, they should take heart. In the 'lawsuit' they will find themselves in (not necessarily specific occasions of being brought before courts, but the heavenly lawsuit Jesus is

81

imagining, in which they will be pitted against 'the world'), the 'helper' will do the job of advocate. The spirit will prove that the world is in the wrong, on the three counts that really matter.

First, the spirit will demonstrate that the world is wrong in relation to sin. In other words, the world is guilty of sin; and the evidence is that 'the world', as we have seen throughout this book, has not believed in Jesus. This can only be, Jesus insists, because it is bent on its own way rather than God's way.

Second, the spirit will demonstrate that the world is wrong in relation to justice. The world thinks it has justice on its side. But the vindication of Jesus himself – which consists of his 'going away' and being exalted to the father – is the sign, as in Daniel 7, that the living God has already given sentence on his behalf. If it's justice you want, we already know the verdict: God has decided in favour of Jesus as the righteous one. All those who follow Jesus share that verdict. (This is where John comes very close to what Paul means by 'justification by **faith**'.)

Third, the spirit will demonstrate that the world is wrong in relation to judgment, which here means 'condemnation'. The world supposes that it can and should pass judgment on Jesus' followers. But the events which are about to unfold, the events of Jesus' death and **resurrection**, indicate decisively that they are wrong. These events mean that 'the ruler of this world' – the dark power that has kept humans and the world enslaved – has been condemned. His power has been broken. Death itself, the weapon of tyrants and particularly of '**the satan**', is a beaten foe.

Now at last we see how it is that 'the advocate' is also 'the comforter'. Because the holy spirit will do all these things, those who suffer persecution and hatred for the name of Jesus can trust that the judge of all the earth will do what is right. But, at the same time, all this comes as a challenge. *How* will the spirit do it? Will it not be, at least in part, through the

82

people in whom 'the helper' comes to live? Will it not, at least in part, be through their speaking out, under the spirit's guidance, on behalf of those suffering injustice and oppression?

JOHN 16.12–22

Your Hearts Will Rejoice

[12]'There are many things I still have to say to you,' Jesus continued, 'but you're not yet strong enough to take them. [13]When the spirit of truth comes, though, he will guide you in all the truth. He won't speak on his own account, you see, but he will speak whatever he hears. He will announce to you what's to come. [14]He will glorify me, because he will take what belongs to me and will announce it to you. [15]Everything that the father has is mine. That's why I said that he would take what is mine and announce it to you.

[16]'Not long from now, you won't see me any more. Then again, not long after that, you will see me!'

[17]'What's he talking about?' some of his disciples asked each other. 'What's this business about "not long from now, you won't see me, and again not long after that you will see me"? And what's this about "going to the father"?'

[18]They kept on saying it.

'What is this "not long"?'

'What's it all about?'

'We don't know what he means!'

[19]Jesus knew that they wanted to ask him.

'You're discussing with each other what I meant, aren't you?' he said. 'You want to know what I meant by saying "Not long from now, you won't see me; and then again, not long after that, you will see me." That's it, isn't it? [20]Well, I'm going to tell you the solemn truth.

'You will weep and wail, but the world will celebrate. You will be overcome with sorrow, but your sorrow will turn into joy. [21]When a woman is giving birth she is in anguish, because her moment has come. But when the child is born, she doesn't remember the suffering, because of the joy that a human being has been born into the world. ²²In the same way, you have sorrow now. But I shall see you again, and your hearts will celebrate, and nobody will take your celebration away from you.'

How do you talk about things that are not just out of the ordinary but that take you into a whole new world?

One way of doing it is through music. That's why some of the greatest songs are love poems. Faced with the glory and thrill of human love, all our words seem threadbare and inadequate. Set them to music, though, and they soar with the eagles and beat in time to our excited hearts.

That's why, too, from very early on in Israel and the church (and elsewhere, of course), people have used music to 'say' things that the words by themselves couldn't do, the things that have to do with the arrival of a whole new world.

Much of the New Testament has from time to time been set to music. A favourite piece in my family is the one in which the nineteenth-century composer Johannes Brahms set the words of verse 22. 'You have sorrow now. But I shall see you again, and your hearts will celebrate.' It is a soaring, gentle but powerful affirmation of joy coming through sorrow and out the other side. It is a rich embodiment of this text, which has again and again been cherished by Christians at times of great distress and suffering. The music has comforted many people who didn't even know what words Brahms was setting, or where they had come from.

Brahms was responding to the theme which lies deep within this passage: the theme of God's new world being born out of the womb of the old. Like Paul in Romans 8, Jesus in this passage uses the imagery of giving birth to express what is going to happen, and invites his followers to prepare themselves for a sorrow, and a subsequent lasting joy, that is modelled on the sorrow and joy of a woman going into labour.

Giving birth is terrifying. It involves sharp pain, convulsions, breathing difficulties, a form of agony that mere men can only watch with awe. But most women giving birth go through it with eager expectation. Their hearts are already set on the new young life that's waiting to come into the world. Within minutes, or even moments, of the birth (assuming they and the child are reasonably healthy), they are deeply content. There may be days and weeks of pain to come as the body recovers from its ordeal. But new life has come, and with it new joy.

Jesus' **disciples** are about to be plunged into a short, sharp and intensely painful period that will be like a moment of birth. Jesus will be taken away; but they will see him again. 'Not long from now, they won't see him; not long after that, they will see him again.' His death and **resurrection** are the necessary events that will lead to his 'going to the father' and his 'sending of the **spirit**'. These are extraordinary, cataclysmic events, the like of which the world has never seen before. The disciples can hardly prepare properly for them; but Jesus wants to warn them anyway.

It's all happening because, with Jesus' death and resurrection, a new world – *the* new world – is indeed being born. That is what John wants us to grasp. This isn't just a matter of Jesus saying 'there's trouble coming, but it will be all right afterwards'. It's a matter of seeing that when we find ourselves, a few chapters from now, at the foot of the cross, and then when we find ourselves after that with Mary Magdalene in the Easter garden, we shouldn't miss the significance of these events. They are not merely strange, shocking and even unique. They are the visible sign that God's new world really is coming to birth.

It's hardly surprising, then, that Jesus has another warning as well. There are all sorts of things he would love to talk to them about which they aren't ready for, which they couldn't cope with. As it is, they are no doubt sleepy at the end of a long day and a festive evening, and he is facing them with warnings and encouragements the like of which the world has never heard before or since.

It's already too much. The funny little dialogue in verses 16–19, with the disciples tossing Jesus' words to and fro, makes that clear enough. No: they won't understand much of it just now. But part of the job of the spirit, the 'helper', will be to lead them into all the truth. The spirit will remind them of what Jesus had already said to them. The spirit will also guide them, nudging their minds and imaginations into ways of knowing, and things to know, that Jesus would like to have said but couldn't at the time.

Maybe we should also say that the spirit will give people music, to make the words take flight in a new way. That, too, is certainly a way by which the father is glorified, as the things to do with Jesus are celebrated. Music can point to that moment, the celebration we are promised, the one nobody can take away from us. Music is, perhaps, not only a signpost to it, but the start of the celebration itself.

JOHN 16.23–33

Ask, and You Will Receive

23'On that day,' Jesus went on, 'you won't ask me for anything. I'm telling you the solemn truth: whatever you ask the father in my name, he will give you. 24Up to now, you haven't asked for anything in my name. Ask, and you will receive, so that your joy may be full!

25'I've been saying all this to you in picture-language. The time is coming when I won't speak in pictures any more. Instead, I'll tell you about the father quite plainly. 26On that day you will ask in my name. I won't say I will ask the father on your behalf, 27because the father himself loves you! That's because you have loved me, and have believed that I came from God. 28I came from the father, and I've come into the world. Now I'm leaving the world, and going back to the father.'

²⁹'Ah!' said his disciples. 'Now you're speaking plainly! You're not talking in pictures. ³⁰Now we know that you know all things, and you don't need to have anybody ask you anything. This makes us trust that you came from God.'

³¹'So you do now believe, do you?' replied Jesus. ³²'Look here: the time is coming (in fact, it's now arrived!) when you will be scattered, each of you to his own place. You will leave me alone – though I'm not alone, because the father is with me. ³³I've said these things to you so that you can have peace in me. You'll have trouble in the world. But cheer up! I have defeated the world!'

In the world of business you can often tell how important someone is by finding out how many people you have to 'go through', as we say, in order to speak to them. You telephone, hoping for a word with the chairman of the company. You get the front desk, who put you through to the main office suite. You get the person at the front of that. She or he puts you through to a secretary. They put you through (if you're lucky) to the Great Man's Personal Assistant. And that's probably it for the day. The Great Man is busy. Or he's in a meeting. Or he's playing golf, or taking a nap (no, they won't say that, but it might be the truth). Three, four or five people to charm your way around, and still you can't get there.

The ancient world was often like that as well. If you came from the country and hoped to see the king or queen, you wouldn't just walk straight in to the royal palace. You would meet a sentry at the gate. Then, if you were allowed past, you would be handed over to a junior official. Then to a gentleman-in-waiting, or near equivalent. Then to a senior official. And so on. Again, you might go through four or five stages, if you were lucky, and still not get near royalty.

But it isn't like that in the **kingdom of God** – despite the best efforts of some Christians to reinvent a system of hierarchies and insist that people should go through them rather than directly to the centre. This passage is all about the fact that Jesus' people have instant, immediate, direct and valued access into the very presence of the living God. Though Jesus, in John's **gospel** and elsewhere, is spoken of as praying to the father on behalf of his people, this doesn't mean that his people can't pray to God themselves, on their own account.

On the contrary. The extraordinary and intimate union between Jesus and the father, which is one of the main subjects of this whole book, means that those who belong to Jesus, the branches who belong in the vine, are granted the same immediate access to the father that Jesus himself has. What is more, when they pray in Jesus' name – which means, as we saw, when they pray conscious of the fact that they belong to him, and that what they are doing is for his glory – then the father welcomes them instantly and gives them whatever they ask for. *Whatever*. There it is again (verse 23).

The reason for this is clear in verse 27: the father himself loves you. Time to throw out of the junk-room of our minds all those medieval images of a distant, remote, uncaring 'father' who has to be pleaded with and, as it were, bribed with the blood of his own son before he can be made even to think of doing something good for us. Time to throw out, too, any idea that Jesus is a bit remote, so that we have to come to him through a succession of others – saints, martyrs, any of them.

The greatest Christians of old (if we can ever rank them) were people who took promises like this at their face value and were humble enough to believe them. It's really a form of pride that stops us accepting an offer as gracious as this. It would be the crowning irony if we now treated such people in their turn as courtiers in God's palace, whom we had to beg to put in a good word for us. If we tried it, they would know what answer to give. The throne-room door is open, they would say. Why not go in and talk to father for yourself?'

This whole passage, then, is about the father: how much he loves each one who trusts in Jesus, and how great are the promises that he makes, in Jesus, to each of us. The **disciples**, listening to these words at the end of these great discourses, have a sense that Jesus is finally speaking as clearly and openly as it's possible to speak about the father, and about himself. They have, at least, glimpsed something of the truth, and they are going to hang on to it for dear life.

They had better do so, because they are about to be tossed to and fro like timber in a tidal wave. The horrible events that Jesus has up to now hinted at and interpreted in various ways are about to engulf him and them. Their initial reaction will be panic and flight. They will be scattered like sheep without a shepherd. Jesus, the shepherd, will face the foe alone – though even then he won't be alone; what he does on the cross he does with and in the father's presence, not over against him.

But the last word isn't one of warning. It's one of good cheer. Somehow, even in the worst that is to come, the disciples can have a peace that will carry them through. This peace doesn't come from a detached, philosophical attitude. It isn't a matter of saying, 'Oh well, these things happen.' It isn't a shrug of the shoulders, resigning yourself to the world being a nasty place and there being nothing much you can do about it. It's a matter of standing on the ground that Jesus is going to win – indeed, that here he claims to have won already. 'You'll have trouble in the world; but cheer up, I've defeated the world!'

Yes. 'The world' that will hate, persecute and ridicule Jesus' followers has been not sidelined, not downgraded, but *defeated*. When Jesus took upon himself the weight of the world's sin; when he burst through death itself into God's new creation; and, already, when he decisively challenged the power of corruption, decay and death in healing the cripple, the man born blind and Lazarus; in and through all these things, he was not just proving a point but winning a victory. Not just setting an example but establishing a new reality. Just as tactically minded politicians like to establish 'facts on the ground' from which they can then launch a new programme, so Jesus has established, and in the coming three days will set up for ever, facts on the ground, kingdom-facts within the history of the world, which are set to become the new order, the way everything will one day be.

JOHN 17.1–8

Glorify the Son

[1]After Jesus had said this, he lifted up his eyes to heaven.

'Father,' he said, 'the moment has come. Glorify your son, so that your son may glorify you. [2]Do this in the same way as you gave him authority over all people, so that he could give eternal life to everyone you gave him. [3]And by "eternal life" I mean this: that they should know you, the one true God, and Jesus the Messiah, the one you sent.

[4]'I glorified you on earth, by completing the work you gave me to do. [5]So now, father, glorify me, alongside yourself, with the glory which I had with you before the world existed.

[6]'I revealed your name to the people you gave me out of the world. They belonged to you; you gave them to me; and they have kept your word. [7]Now they know that everything which you gave me comes from you. [8]I have given them the words you gave me, and they have received them. They have come to know, in truth, that I came from you. They have believed that you sent me.'

Shakespeare's play *Hamlet* is full of action. Ghosts, murders, love scenes, plots, accidental killings, betrayals, recriminations and more plots. The play highlights the indecision of the hero when faced with huge problems, and this results in pauses here and there. But at one moment in particular the action comes to a shuddering halt.

Hamlet is looking for an opportunity to take revenge on his stepfather, Claudius, for murdering his father and usurping the throne of Denmark. He comes upon an ideal opportunity: Claudius is in his chamber, kneeling quietly. But Hamlet stops, and thinks. Claudius is praying! If he takes revenge now, Claudius may perhaps have repented and will be saved. Hamlet decides to wait for a better moment. The sorry tale continues.

He is praying! There is a mystery there which nobody can penetrate except the one who is doing the praying. Just as I cannot be sure that when you see something red you are seeing exactly the same colour as I am, so I cannot be sure what passes between you and God when you kneel down and pray. Hamlet couldn't tell what Claudius was praying, but knew he should pause and wait. And, with a totally different king, equally caught up in mystery, intrigue and plots but innocent of all, we come in this chapter to a place where we, too, should pause and wait, and perhaps quietly join in.

Jesus is praying! Of course, we know that Jesus prayed. The **gospels** tell us that frequently. But they hardly ever tell us what he prayed or how he prayed. A few sentences at most come down to us, such as that wonderful passage in Matthew (11.25–27), and the burst of praise at the tomb of Lazarus (John 11.41–42). Interestingly, both of those passages look remarkably like shorter versions of what we find in this outstanding, ecstatic chapter. I once heard an actor read the whole of John's gospel, and when he came to this chapter he knelt down and prayed it as a prayer. It sounded, and *felt*, like prayer. This is not simply a theological treatise, with John putting ideas together and placing them on Jesus' lips.

Nor, we may suppose, is John remembering it all without having prayed through it himself, over and over again. The mention of 'Jesus the **Messiah**' in verse 3 sounds very strange from Jesus himself; perhaps here, and maybe elsewhere too, John the praying teacher, in order to make the prayer his own and pass it on to his own followers, has turned phrases round so that they become (so to speak) prayable by the continuing community. But in essence the prayer draws together everything that the gospel story has been about up to this point.

In particular, the very fact of Jesus' prayer is a living embodiment of that intimate union with the father of which we have heard so much. I remember the first time, as a young musician, that I sat in the middle of a school orchestra and played my small part with the music *happening all round me*, instead of coming at me from the loudspeaker of a radio or gramophone. When you make this prayer your own, when you enter into this chapter and see what happens, you are being invited to come into the heart of that intimate relation between Jesus and the father and have it, so to speak, happen all round you. That is both what the prayer embodies and also its central subject matter.

This first section of the prayer is a celebration and a request. The two are closely linked. Jesus is celebrating the fact that his work is done. Yes, there is the huge and awful task awaiting him the next day. But he has completed the deeds and words which the father gave him to do. (Those who see Jesus as simply a great teacher, or think that his task was to heal as many as possible, naturally find this a puzzle.) He has laid before his chosen **disciples** all that the father has given to him. That is the reason for the celebration, and it is the ground of the request he now makes.

His request is that he may now be exalted, glorified, lifted up to that position alongside the father which in Jewish tradition the king, the Messiah, the **son of man**, was supposed to attain. The Messiah, say the psalms, will rule a **kingdom** that stretches from sea to sea, from 'the River' to 'the ends of the earth' (Psalm 72.8). In other words, he will have a universal dominion. 'One like a son of man' will be exalted to share the throne of God himself (Daniel 7).

When the Messiah takes his seat, exalted over the world, then the **age to come** will truly have begun – that 'coming age' which Jewish prophets longed for, which Jewish sages taught would appear at the end of 'the **present age**'. It would be the time of new **life**, life with a new quality (not just quantity, going on and on for ever). It would be, in our inadequate phrase, '**eternal life**'.

This 'eternal life', this life of the coming age, is not just something which people can have after their death. It isn't simply that in some future state the world will go on for ever and ever and we shall be part of it. The point is, rather, that this new sort of life has come to birth in the world in and through Jesus. Once he has completed the final victory over death itself, all his followers, all who trust him and believe that he has truly come from the father, and has truly unveiled the father's character and purpose – all of them can and will possess 'eternal life' right here and now. That, too, has been one of the great themes of this gospel (e.g. 3.16; 5.24).

So far, the prayer may seem far too exalted for us to join in. But, as we shall see in the next two sections, the relationship between Jesus and the father, though it seems extraordinarily close and trusting, is not designed to be exclusive. We are invited to join in.

JOHN 17.9–19

Jesus Prays for His People

⁹'I'm praying for them. I'm not praying for the world, but for the people you've given me. They belong to you. ¹⁰All mine are yours; all yours are mine; and I'm glorified in them.

¹¹'I'm not in the world any longer, but they're still in the

world; I'm coming to you. Holy father, keep them in your name, the name you've given to me, so that they may be one, just as we are one.

[12]'When I was with them, I kept them in your name, the name you've given me. I guarded them, and none of them has been lost (except the son of destruction; that's what the Bible said would happen). [13]But now I'm coming to you. I'm speaking these things in the world, so that they can have my joy fulfilled in them.

[14]'I have given them your word. The world hated them, because they haven't come from the world, just as I didn't come from the world. [15]I'm not asking that you should take them out of the world, but that you should keep them from the evil one. [16]They didn't come from the world, just as I didn't come from the world. [17]Make them holy in the truth; your word is truth. [18]Just as you sent me into the world, so I sent them into the world. [19]And on their account I set myself apart for you, so that they, too, may be set apart for you in the truth.'

In the newspapers recently a mother was punished by the courts. She had left her two young children entirely by themselves, while she went off for a foreign holiday with her new boyfriend. (The father, it seems, was nowhere to be found.) It is hard to believe that a mother could do such a thing. One wonders what she thought she would find when she got home. Tragically, such things happen in our world today.

But supposing she herself had had loving parents who were only too glad to look after the children while she was away? That would have made all the difference. She could have entrusted the little ones to them, safe in the knowledge that they would care for them as much as she did. One can imagine a mother in that situation giving her parents detailed instructions as to how each child should be looked after, not because she didn't trust her parents to look after them but because she did.

What Jesus now prays grows out of the fact that he is going away. He is entrusting the **disciples** to the father he has known and loved throughout his own earthly life, the father who, he knows, will care for them every bit as much as he has done himself. He is very much aware that the disciples are at risk. The world, which hates them as it hated him, will threaten and abuse them. They don't belong to it, but they are to be sent into it, and they need protecting. That's what the prayer is about.

This section begins with a description of who Jesus' followers are. They are the ones the father has given to Jesus; they already belong to him, and Jesus is handing them back into his safe keeping. They are distinct from 'the world'. Insofar as they are the new, cleansed people they have become through Jesus' call and teaching (see 15.3), they are not 'from the world'.

This can seem puzzling, and we'd better explain it a bit more. Jesus is not suggesting that his followers don't possess human ancestry, homes and families, and physical bodies which will one day decay and die. 'The world', remember, in this **gospel** doesn't mean simply the physical universe as we know it. It means the world insofar as it has rebelled against God, has chosen darkness rather than light, and has organized itself to oppose the creator. Seen from within that 'world', Jesus is 'from' elsewhere. So too, we now discover to our surprise, are the disciples. In other words, 'the world' in this dark sense is not the place, the force, the sphere, that determines who the disciples most truly are.

What they now need, therefore, is to be kept from being pulled back into 'the world' with all its wickedness and rebellion. During his public ministry, teaching them and leading them, Jesus has looked after them, like the shepherd with his sheep. (He mentions, with sorrow, the loss of one sheep, though with the recognition that there was an inevitability about it. The Bible had said it would happen, as we saw in 13.18.) Now, because he is coming to the father, he is entrusting them to the father, who will continue the work of keeping them safe.

He therefore addresses the father as 'holy' (verse 11), and declares that he is 'setting himself apart' so that the disciples too may be 'set apart'. The word for 'setting apart' is basically the same as the word for 'holy'; but our word 'holy', when applied to people, can give a sense of over-pious religiosity which is foreign to the New Testament. What is 'holiness' in Jesus' world?

In first-century Judaism, 'holiness' called to mind the **Temple** in particular. It was the holy place, the place where the holy God had promised to live. It referred particularly to the Holy of Holies, the innermost shrine, where the **high priest** would go once a year to make atonement for the people. The high priest had to go through special ceremonies of 'consecration', to be 'set apart' so that he could enter into the presence of the holy God, and pray there for his people. In exactly the same way, Jesus is declaring that he has been, all along, 'set apart', 'consecrated' for God's exclusive service. Now, like the high priest, he is asking the father to preserve his people from evil, from the tricks and traps of 'the world'. He wants them to be his holy people in the best and fullest sense.

What Jesus has already done for them is to 'keep' them in the father's name (verse 12) and to give them his **word** (verse 14). In other words, when he now entrusts them to the father, this won't mean a sudden change, like a mother entrusting her children to someone of whom they've never heard and whose house will be run on quite different lines to their own home. He has already taught them, so to speak, the table manners appropriate for the father's house. In praying for them now, he is simply praying that what he has begun, the father will gloriously complete.

This prayer has been used for many centuries by pastors, teachers and other Christian leaders as they pray for those in their care. It can also, with only slight variation, be used by Christians of all sorts for themselves. Substitute 'Jesus' where the prayer says 'I', and replace 'they' and 'them' with 'I' and 'me', and you'll get the idea. But be careful. This is a serious prayer. It is one of the most serious things Jesus ever said. That's why, deep down, it is also among the most joyful and hopeful. Pray it with awe, and with delight.

JOHN 17.20–26

That They May Be One

[20]'I'm not simply praying for them. I'm praying, too, for the people who will come to believe in me because of their word. [21]I am praying that they may all be one – just as you, father, are in me, and I in you, that they too may be in us, so that the world may believe that you sent me.

[22]'I have given them the glory which you have given to me, so that they may be one, just as we are one. [23]I in them, and you in me; yes, they must be completely one, so that the world may know that you sent me, and that you loved them just as you loved me.

[24]'Father, I want the ones you've given me to be with me where I am. I want them to see my glory, the glory which you've given me, because you loved me before the foundation of the world.

[25]'Righteous father, even the world didn't know you. But I have known you, and these ones have known that you sent me. [26]I made your name known to them – yes, and I will make it known; so that the love with which you loved me may be in them, and I in them.'

This afternoon I looked on the Internet for a website about an electric appliance that's gone wrong. I've lost the instruction booklet and was hoping to find relevant information through the Web.

I found the website of the company that makes the appliance and looked for information about it. I then spotted that there was a special category entitled 'Frequently Asked Questions'. FAQs for short. Exactly what I needed . . .

In the church where I work, people come from all over the world. Many of them have never been in an Anglican (Episcopal) church before. Our most frequently asked question comes because they are puzzled by what we say every day during worship, in the words of one of the creeds (the great statements of belief produced by the early Christians). What puzzles them is when we say that we believe in the 'one, holy, catholic and apostolic church'. Surely, they say on the way out, you are Anglicans, not Catholics? Why do you say you believe in the 'catholic' church?

The answer is that the word 'catholic' simply means 'universal'. Of course, many people say 'catholic' when what they strictly mean is 'Roman Catholic'. That's where the confusion arises. But, since many people, including many practising Christians, don't often think about what the church actually is, and why, this gives an opportunity to say something more. And this section, the end of Jesus' great prayer, is where a good deal of our view of the church comes from.

Imagine some great figure of the past. Shakespeare, perhaps. George Washington, possibly. Socrates. Think of someone you respect and admire. Now imagine that the historians have just found, among old manuscripts, a letter from the great man himself. And imagine that it was talking about . . . you. How would you feel?

That is how you should feel as you read verse 20. Jesus is talking about *you*. And me. 'Those who believe in me through their word', that is, through the word of his followers. His followers announced the **message** around the world. Those who heard them passed it on. And on, and on, and on. The church is never more than one generation away from extinction; all it would take is for a single generation not to hand the **word** on. But it's never happened. People have always told other people. I am writing this book, and you are reading it, as a result. It's awesome, when you come to think about it.

But what is Jesus praying for, as he thinks about you and me and all his other followers in this and every generation? He is praying that we may be, just as the old words say, 'one, holy and universal,' founded on the teaching of the followers, the '**apostles**', the ones who were with him on that occasion. In particular, he longed that we should all be one. United.

This unity isn't to be just a formal arrangement. It isn't just an outward thing. It is based on, and must mirror, nothing less than the unity between the father and the son, that unity that much of the book has been explaining and exploring. Just as the father is in the son, and the son in the father, so we too are to live within that unity. That can only mean that we ourselves are to be united. And, in case we might miss the point, the result of this will be that the world will see, and know, that this kind of human community, united across all traditional barriers of race, custom, gender or class, can only come from the action of the creator God. 'So that the world may believe . . .'

Notice how this picks up what Jesus said in 13.35. 'This is how all people will know that you are my **disciples**: if you have love for each other.' Unity is vital. Often we sense it, heard like soft music through the partition walls we set up around ourselves. Sometimes we experience it, when for a moment we meet Christians from a totally different background and discover that, despite our many differences, and the traditions that keep us apart, we know a unity of love and devotion that cannot be broken. But just as often, alas, we experience, sense and know that Jesus' prayer for us has not yet been fully answered.

As in any human relationship, unity cannot be forced. There can be no bullying, no manipulation. But in a divided world, where the divisions have often run down so-called 'religious' lines, there is no excuse for Christians not to work afresh in every generation towards the unity Jesus prayed for. If we are, essentially, one in **faith**, there can be no final reason why we may not be one, also, in our life and worship.

In addition, Jesus returns to an earlier theme (see 12.26 and 14.3). His followers are to be 'with him', to see his glory. They are to know and experience the fact that the father has exalted him as the sovereign of the world. They are to know that the love which the creator God has given to him has installed him as the loving Lord of all.

Many Christians today draw back from that statement. (We spoke about this problem earlier in relation to 14.6.) They suppose, naturally enough, that it will sound arrogant, or as though they are giving themselves a special status by claiming this about Jesus. But this is to misunderstand the whole message of the **gospel**. When Jesus is exalted, the reason is nothing other than love. This is not the sort of sovereignty that enables people to think themselves better than others. It is the sort of sovereignty that commits them, as it committed Jesus, to loving service.

That's what the whole prayer comes down to in the end (verse 26). It is about the love of the father surrounding Jesus, and this same love, as a bond and badge, surrounding all Jesus' people, making him present to them and through them to the world. And, whereas in verse 11 Jesus addressed the father as 'holy', now he addresses him as 'righteous' (verse 25). The father is the judge of all the earth; though the world rages against Jesus' followers, he will see that right will prevail.

But, as always in the New Testament, the justice for which we pray, the righteous judgment through which the father expresses himself in his world, appears before us as love. That is because, supremely, it appears before us in the person of Jesus. It is this Jesus, this man who prayed for you and me, this

high priest who set himself apart for the father's glad service, whom we shall now watch as he goes forward to complete the work of love.

JOHN 18.1–14

The Arrest of Jesus

[1]With these words, Jesus went out with his disciples across the Kidron valley to a place where there was a garden. He and his disciples went in.

[2]Judas, his betrayer, knew the place, because Jesus often used it as a meeting-place with his disciples. [3]So Judas took a band of soldiers, with some servants of the chief priests and the Pharisees, and came there with torches, lights and weapons.

[4]Jesus knew exactly what was going to happen to him. He went out to meet them.

'Who are you looking for?' he asked.

[5]'Jesus of Nazareth,' they answered.

'I'm the one,' he said to them.

Judas, his betrayer, was standing there with them. [6]So when he said, 'I'm the one,' they went back a few paces, and fell down on the ground.

[7]Jesus repeated his question.

'Who are you looking for?' he asked.

'Jesus of Nazareth,' they said.

[8]'I told you, I'm the one!' said Jesus. 'So, if you're looking for me, let these people go.' ([9]He said this so as to fulfil the word he had spoken, when he said, 'I haven't lost any of the people you gave me.')

[10]Simon Peter had a sword. He drew it and hit the high priest's servant, cutting off his right ear. The servant's name was Malchus.

[11]'Put your sword back in its sheath!' said Jesus to Peter. 'Do you imagine I'm not going to drink the cup my father has given me?'

> ¹²So the band of soldiers, with the officer and the Judaean attendants, arrested Jesus and tied him up. ¹³They led him off first to Annas; he was the father-in-law of Caiaphas, who was high priest that year. ¹⁴It was Caiaphas who had given advice to the Judaeans that the best thing would be for one man to die for the people.

He came, looking for someone. He came on the evening breeze, came as he had always come. Came because they knew each other, and used to spend time together. Came to the garden, because that's where they always met. That's where he was at home.

And there was no answer. The man had hidden. Something had happened. The friendship was soured. There was a bad taste in the air, a taste made worse by the excuses and feeble stories that followed. Love, the most fragile and beautiful of the plants in that garden, had been trampled on. It would take millennia to grow it again.

The story of Adam in the garden, in Genesis 2 and 3, stands behind the garden of betrayal in this chapter as well as the garden of Easter in chapter 20. John is, after all, writing a kind of 'new Genesis', as we saw at the beginning. He hasn't forgotten that, even if we may have. Now, in this extraordinary and decisive scene, we see what it means that the **Word** became *flesh*: our flesh, Adam's flesh, new-Genesis flesh.

The roles are reversed. Sinful men, violent men, men with weapons, come to the garden in the dark, looking for someone. The someone who was the father's only son. Like all humans, they are looking for God, but they don't know that's what they are doing. They think they are only doing their job . . .

Jesus doesn't hide. He has no reason to. The father has given him a cup to drink, and he's going to drink it. The agony in the garden, so movingly pictured in Matthew, Mark and especially Luke, is missing from John. John has shown us already how, three times over, Jesus' heart has been deeply troubled (11.33; 12.27; 13.21). The moment has now passed. He is ready. The new Adam steps forward to meet the old; the Word who was and is God comes to greet 'the world'; the light of the world stands before those who, in their darkness, have come with torches and lanterns. The light shines in the darkness, and the darkness is not going to extinguish it.

The scene becomes still more extraordinary as it progresses. Jesus takes the initiative and asks them who they are looking for. They tell him. His answer is simple and shocking: 'I AM'. In the setting, of course, this means, 'I'm the one', or, 'That's me'. But for John, with the God-and-Adam confrontation in the background, and all the 'I AM' sayings throughout his book in the foreground, there is no doubt what he wants us to hear.

This is the simple, clear and world-changing statement: the vulnerable man standing before you in the garden, glimpsed in the flickering torchlight, is the one who from all eternity was equal with the father. He is the I AM, the bread of **life**, the light of the world, the **resurrection** and the life, the way, the truth and the life. Something of this is the only reasonable explanation why, in this version, the arresting party stumble backwards and fall to the ground. (Unless, that is, we are to say that this is a moment of sheer comedy, with the soldiers tripping over one another in the dark.) Their reaction, whether voluntary or involuntary, mirrors what people in the Bible do when coming face to face with God.

What, after all, might it look like if the Jesus of John 13—17 were to come out of the upper room, after the meal with the **disciples**, the footwashing, the sublime discourses and the prayer, and were to stand facing 'the world'? Would you expect him to wave a magic wand and win a cheap victory? Would you expect him to lead a military revolution? Of course not (though Peter, clearly, was still thinking like that; putting his thoughtless action alongside Jesus' denial of military intent in 18.36 gives us plenty to think about, not least the sense that, as with the first Eden, bloodshed is the sorry sign of human failure). Rather, you would expect him to be calm, however troubled his heart might have been in previous days or that very evening; you would expect him to offer no resistance; you would expect him to stay in command both of his own followers (the order to Peter) and indeed of those who had come to arrest him (the order to the soldiers to let the rest go, in verse 8).

And you would expect the whole scene to be heavy with the irony that will continue until we arrive at the foot of the cross. Jesus, who has just completed his great prayer as the true **high priest** of God's renewed Israel, is now taken before Annas, the senior member of the high priestly family, with his son-in-law Caiaphas among those present. And John reminds us what Caiaphas had said, back in 11.49–50.

We now know, if there had been any doubt, what is going to happen and what it means. The true high priest will be sent to his death by the false one, so that through his death God will rescue his people. The true Adam will be sent to his death by the false ones, so that the garden may be restored, and instead of bloodshed there may be healing and forgiveness. The Word who was and is God is led away for questioning by God's official representative.

I don't know that any of us will ever be able to hold all this in our minds at any one time. John allows the images to build up, one upon another upon another, until we're overwhelmed by them. That's part of the point. You can no more read this story at one level only, a simple arrest and trial, than you can plant a garden in a coffee cup. The only way forward is to allow all the different ideas and levels, the clashes of meaning and misunderstanding, to echo around until they produce prayer, awe, silence and love.

JOHN 18.15–27

Peter Denies Jesus

[15]Simon Peter and another disciple followed Jesus. That other disciple was known to the high priest; he went in to the high priest's courtyard along with Jesus, [16]while Peter stood outside by the gate. So the other disciple, being known to the high priest, went out and spoke to the woman on the gate. Then he brought Peter inside.

[17]The woman on the gate spoke to Peter.

'You're not one of that man's disciples, are you?' she asked.

'No, I'm not,' he replied.

[18]It was cold. The slaves and the attendants had made a charcoal fire, and they were standing round it, warming themselves. Peter was standing there with them and warming himself.

[19]The high priest asked Jesus about his disciples, and about his teaching.

[20]'I've spoken to the world quite openly,' replied Jesus. 'I always taught in the synagogue and in the Temple, where all the Judaeans gather. I didn't say anything in secret. [21]Why are you asking me? There were people who listened to me. Ask them what I said to them. Don't you see? They know what I said.'

[22]When Jesus said that, one of the attendants standing there gave him a slap on the face.

'Is that how you answer the high priest?' he said.

[23]'If I've said something wrong,' replied Jesus, 'give evidence about what was wrong with it. But if what I said was true, why are you hitting me?'

[24]So Annas sent him off, still tied up, to Caiaphas the high priest.

[25]Simon Peter, meanwhile, was standing there and warming himself.

'You're not one of his disciples, are you?' they asked him.

He denied it. 'No, I'm not,' he said.

[26]Then one of the high priest's slaves, a relative of the man whose ear Peter had cut off, spoke up.

'Didn't I see you in the garden with him?' he said.
²⁷Peter denied it once more. Instantly, the cock crowed.

There is a part of the human brain which seems to be closed off for much of the time, but which can be reached at once through the sense of smell. You can be walking down the street, thinking of something completely different, when a single sniff of someone's pipe tobacco, or a single breath from a particular tree in a garden, can take you back twenty years or more to a memory you didn't even know you had. You can recall the place, the people, what was said, and particularly what it *felt* like. Many animals have much better senses of smell than we do; but ours is – well, I was going to say it's not to be sneezed at. You will understand what I mean.

There is one feature of this sad story, the story of Peter telling people he didn't belong to Jesus when his heart was crying out that he really did, which comes into this category. Charcoal fires have a particular smell to them; I can't possibly describe it, but you'd know it if you smelt it again. And you'd remember what you were doing, and what was said, last time you came upon one. Well, not very long after this, there is another charcoal fire that comes into the story (21.9). It calls up for Peter, and for Jesus, the memory of this sad night. And it does so (this is the way the **gospel** of Jesus works, after all), in order to heal the open wound that this sorry tale has left in Peter, and perhaps in Jesus as well.

As in Mark's gospel, the story of Peter's denial is woven together with the story of Jesus' interrogation by the senior **priests**. It's not quite clear here whether it's Caiaphas, the actual **high priest** that year, who's doing the questioning, or whether it's Annas, Caiaphas's father-in-law. Caiaphas was most probably there at Annas's house for the initial exchange, and it may be that Annas sent Jesus on to Caiaphas's house (verse 24) for a more formal interrogation, such as the one we find in the other gospels. Some ancient copies of the gospels actually moved some of the verses in this passage around to try to make more sense of the movements to and fro. Perhaps part of the point is that it was all very confused, very dark and very frightening, and nobody quite knew what was going on.

Anyway, we now find Jesus speaking quite firmly to the high priest – and getting slapped in the face for his pains. But the main focus of the story remains on Peter. Jesus is telling the high priest the truth while Peter is telling lies to the servants. Jesus is speaking openly, Peter is doing his best to hide. Yet at least he's there, unlike all the rest – except for the 'other **disciple**' of verses 15 and 16. (Who is this? What's he doing there? Why didn't they ask him if he was one of Jesus' followers? How did he come to be known to the high priest? Was he, perhaps, too young for them to worry about? Was he, perhaps, the beloved disciple himself? Another puzzle in the dark night.) But Peter has come for all the right, and all the wrong, reasons.

He's come because he's loyal; but he had never understood more than half of what Jesus was saying, and it's the half he hasn't understood that is going to let him down now. He is cold and tired, drained of the sudden rush of energy in the garden. He must know that if the guards realized he'd not only been there, but had maimed one of the high priest's servants with that senseless swish of his sword, then Jesus might well have the company of his senior associate as he went to meet his fate – something Jesus was at pains to avoid. But all these thoughts come together and produce fear, panic, lies and disloyalty.

John tells the story simply and without adornment. He doesn't even say, as the others do, that Peter went out and burst into tears. But by the time we reach verse 27, if we have been living inside Peter's skin through the previous passage, that's what we want to do as well. He will need all the gentle but probing pastoral wisdom of the good shepherd before this hurt is healed.

~~Jesus, meanwhile, is quizzed about his disciples and his~~ teaching. That's standard practice. If, today, they catch someone they think is a terrorist leader, they want to know exactly what he's been saying and teaching, and who his closest associates are. Jesus won't give them any help with finding his followers, but when it comes to his teaching, he is hardly going to start giving them a résumé of everything he's said over the past two or three years. Nobody in a hastily convened night hearing would be in the mood to listen to **parables**, and much that he has said can only be said that way. They weren't ready for a careful explanation of the ways in which the **kingdom of God** both is and isn't coming, the difference between the normal revolution of Jesus' contemporaries and the radically different revolution he was pioneeering. Go and ask the people who heard me, he says. They'll tell you.

The slap on the face goes with Peter's slicing off the servant's ear. Violence has begun, and will escalate from here. But, already, Jesus has begun to take the rebuke that his follower had earned. The cock has crowed to remind Peter of promises broken, and of Jesus' accurate prediction (13.38). The morning will bring the fulfilment of other predictions, too. The **son of man** will face the ruler of this world, or at least his official representative. The light will shine once more into the darkness.

JOHN 18.28–32

Pilate and the Judaeans

²⁸So they took Jesus from Caiaphas to the governer's residence. It was early in the morning. They didn't themselves go inside the residence. They were anxious not to pollute themselves, so that they would still be able to eat the Passover.

²⁹So Pilate went outside and spoke to them.

'What's the charge, then?' he asked. 'What have you got against this fellow?'

[30]'If he wasn't doing wicked things,' they replied, 'we wouldn't have handed him over to you.'

[31]'Take him yourselves,' said Pilate to them, 'and judge him by your own law.'

'We're not allowed to put anyone to death,' replied the Judaeans. [32](This was so that the word of Jesus might come true, when he had indicated what sort of death he was going to die.)

I watched today as the television interviewer fired questions at a man whose main aim seemed to be to answer them all at great length without saying anything at all. On and on the interviewer went, trying angle after angle; but the man stood his ground. No, he repeated, our policy is such-and-such. Our main aim is to make sure that all the different interests of the region are balanced as best as can be. Yes, compromises will be needed (though he never said what). No, we don't intend to impose our own solution, but to help the region find its own. And so on. And so on.

The man was a special envoy to a part of the Middle East that has been under huge stress and pressure in recent days. (Sadly, that sentence could have been written at any time in the last century or so, and I suspect it will still feel up to date for a long time to come.) He had gone from his home in the comfortable and affluent part of the world to represent the Western powers, or some of them, in an inhospitable and hostile land, where people spoke a different language not only with their lips but with their hearts and lives. Things were different there. If he could only keep things quiet, prevent trouble, present a good front to people back home, hope that no major disaster brewed up . . .

And of course that describes Pontius Pilate as well. He was a long way from home. (Some traditions suggest he was born in Scotland, but we have no way of checking that.) He was a career politician, perhaps, or a soldier who had risen to be a provincial governor, though a junior one. He probably hoped that an effective tour of duty in Judaea would lead to better things: senior postings, better pay and if possible an easier local situation to deal with.

It was not to be. He was eventually removed from office after the Judaeans accused him of all kinds of arrogant, bullying and offensive behaviour. Apart from much later legends, he vanishes from history in about AD 37.

His policy seems to have revolved around two aims in particular. On the one hand, he wanted to keep things quiet in the turbulent Middle East. His bosses, back in Rome, needed a steady corn supply from Egypt; without that, food would run short in the overcrowded and underemployed streets of Rome itself, and major trouble would result. In the first century, as in the twenty-first, the Western powers depended on resources from the Middle East, and needed some measure of peace and stability in what was then as now a turbulent region. It was Pilate's aim, by sheer brutality where necessary, to keep the lid down on what could become a boiling political pot.

On the other hand, he seems to have taken delight in snubbing the Jewish people, and particularly their leaders, whenever he could. If they very much wanted something to happen, he would take pride in thwarting them. If there was something they didn't want, he might well do it. He needed to show them that he was in charge and that they depended on him.

These two aims determined the way Pilate behaved throughout the following scenes. Though he was the official representative of Roman 'justice', that quality seems to have been interpreted, as in some other similar situations, with considerable flexibility. It all boiled down to pragmatism. To what would work.

This is why, to begin with, he didn't want anything to do

with the chief **priests**, fussing at him on the morning of a festival, refusing to come into his official residence so they wouldn't incur ritual pollution. (John, we note, loses no chance to remind us once again that this is Passover; the lambs are being prepared for **sacrifice** in the **Temple** as Jesus is brought before the Roman governor who has sole power over life and death.)

The chief priests are evasive. 'He's doing wicked things.' They know, and Pilate may well know (Roman governors had networks of spies, and it's quite likely that Pilate knew at least as much about Jesus as the chief priests did), that Jesus wasn't actually stirring up a real, military-style revolution. But they wanted him out of the way, for reasons that we have seen over and over again in John's story, culminating with the cynical policy stated by Caiaphas in 11.49–50. Clearly, from the question Pilate asks Jesus in the next section (verse 33), something must have been said, or implied, about Jesus' being a 'king'. The accusers insist that he's guilty of something deserving death. And only the Romans have the legal power to kill people.

In other words, Jesus is going to die the death that Rome reserved for rebels. He had said that he would be 'lifted up', like the serpent in the wilderness (3.14), and that when he was 'lifted up' he would draw all people to himself (12.32). This 'lifting up', for John, has merged into being 'glorified': Jesus on the cross will reveal, in its full extent, the astonishing majesty of God's saving love. But at this point the lines of meaning converge. What Jesus intends, what the chief priests intend, and what Pilate intends, are all rushing together into an event so thickly interwoven that we shall need to peer at it, now from this angle, now from that, until we slowly understand all that John wants to tell us about it.

For the moment, we simply note the marking-signs he has put down. It is Passover. Pilate doesn't want to touch this case. The chief priests are determined that Jesus shall die, and that

Pilate must therefore take charge of the matter. The greatest legal system of the ancient world, and its noblest religion, come together in the centre of the world (as Jerusalem was long supposed), and at the centre of history. Together they blunder and stumble into an act so wicked, so unjust, so unnecessary and so indicative of their own moral bankruptcy that, before anything more is said, we can already draw the correct conclusion. The man at the centre of this storm was indeed dying for the sins of the world.

JOHN 18.33–40

My Kingdom Is Not from This World

[33]So Pilate went back in to the residence and spoke to Jesus.

'Are you the King of the Jews?' he asked.

[34]'Did *you* think of that?' asked Jesus. 'Or did other people tell you about me?'

[35]'I'm not a Jew, am I?' retorted Pilate. 'Your own people, and the chief priests, have handed you over to me! What have you done?'

[36]'My kingdom isn't the sort that grows in this world,' replied Jesus. 'If my kingdom were from this world, my supporters would have fought, to stop me being handed over to the Judaeans. But it's not like that. My kingdom isn't the sort that comes from here.'

[37]'So!' said Pilate. 'You *are* a king, are you?'

'You're calling me a king,' replied Jesus. 'I was born for this; I've come into the world for this: to give evidence about the truth. Everyone who belongs to the truth listens to my voice.'

[38]'Truth!' said Pilate. 'What's that?'

With those words, he went back out to the Judaeans.

'I find this man not guilty!' he said. [39]'But look here: you've got this custom that I should let someone free at Passover-time. So what about it? Would you like me to release "The King of the Jews"?'

⁴⁰'No!' they shouted. 'We don't want him! Give us Barabbas!'

Now Barabbas was a brigand.

The ancient world knew more about kings than we moderns do.

Where kings and queens still exist today, they mostly live and work within a carefully constructed framework. They are not 'absolute' monarchs, but 'constitutional' ones. They can bring subtle pressure to bear on politicians. They can let it be known that they would prefer one course to be followed, rather than another. But let them try anything more than subtle pressure, and people will get restless. Monarchs must now stay within careful limits.

Of course, there are plenty of places in the world where people still rule in an autocratic, dictatorial fashion, without any semblance of democratic consultation. But in the ancient world this was far more widespread. People knew what kings did (and queens too; but since we are talking about Jesus, let's keep it at kings for the moment). Kings ruled people according to their own wishes and whims. They could promote one person and demote another. They were all-powerful.

And people knew how kings became kings, too. Often, the crown would pass from father to son, or to some other close male relative. But from time to time there would be a revolution. The way to the crown, for anyone not in the direct family line, was through violence. This was so among the Jews as much as among the pagans. Judas Maccabaeus had established his dynasty, two hundred years before Jesus met Pilate, through military revolution against the Syrians, winning for the Jews their independence, and for himself and his family a royal status they had not previously aspired to. Herod the Great, thirty years before Jesus was born, had defeated the Parthians, the great empire to the east, and Rome in gratitude had allowed him to become 'King of the Jews', though he, too, had no appropriate background or pedigree.

So when Pilate faces Jesus, and someone hints that the reason the chief **priests** have handed him over is because he thinks he's a king, this must be what he assumes is going on. Pilate doesn't understand, and doesn't want to understand, the ins and outs of the odd ways (as they would seem to him) in which the Jews organize their life. But he knows what kings are, what kingdoms are, where they come from, and how they behave. And he knows that it's his job to allow no such thing on his patch. So out he comes with it. 'Are you the King of the Jews?'

The idea is, of course, so laughable that he knows, within his own frame of reference, what the answer is. He sees before him a poor man from the wrong part of the country. He has a small band of followers and they've all run away. Of course he's not the king. But . . . maybe he thinks he is. Maybe he's really deluded. Better ask him and find out.

Pilate then discovers, as many discovered before him and many have since, that when you ask Jesus a question the answer is likely to be another question. Where is the suggestion coming from? Who put this idea into your head? Pilate waves this away. Don't expect me to understand you peculiar Jews. You must have done something wrong or you wouldn't be here.

Jesus' answer is both apparently incriminating and deeply revealing. His **kingdom** (yes, he agrees he has a kingdom; Pilate seizes on this) doesn't come from this world. Please note, he doesn't say, as some translations have put it, 'my kingdom is not *of* this world'; that would imply that his 'kingdom' was altogether other-worldly, a spiritual or heavenly reality that had nothing to do with the present world at all. That is not the point. Jesus, after all, taught his **disciples** to pray that God's kingdom would come 'on earth as in **heaven**'.

No: the point is that Jesus' kingdom does not come *from*

'this world'. Of course it doesn't. 'The world', as we've seen again and again, is in John the source of evil and rebellion against God. Jesus is denying that his kingdom has a this-worldly *origin* or *quality*. He is not denying that it has a this-worldly *destination*. That's why he has come into the world himself (verse 37), and why he has sent, and will send, his followers into the world (17.18; 20.21). His kingdom doesn't come from this world, but it is for this world. That is the crucial distinction.

In particular, as he points out, if his kingdom were of the normal type, his followers would fight to stop him being handed over. They nearly did, of course, and he had to restrain them (18.10–11); Peter needed to learn the lesson Jesus was now teaching Pilate, and it would take nothing less than the **resurrection** to get it through to him. But Jesus is indeed claiming to be a king, even though he isn't the sort of king that Judas Maccabaeus was, that Herod the Great was, still less the sort that Caesar was. This was why he had come in the first place.

He was, in fact, speaking and bringing the truth. Truth isn't something that you get out of a test tube, or a mathematical formula. We don't have truth in our pockets. Philosophers and judges don't own it. It is a gift, a strange quality that, like Jesus' kingdom in fact, comes from elsewhere but is meant to take up residence in this world. Jesus has come to give evidence about this truth. He is himself the truth.

Pilate, of course, can only see things from a this-worldly perspective. As far as he knows, the only place you get truth is out of the sheath of a sword (or, as we would say, out of the barrel of a gun). Political 'truth'; my truth against your truth, my sword against your sword, with those two meaning much the same thing. And ultimately, for a Roman governor, my truth against your truth, my power against your weakness, my cross to hang your naked body on.

Ah, but that's the truth. The truth that belongs with Passover.

The truth that says one man dies and the others go free. Barabbas, the brigand, perhaps himself either a would-be king or a supporter of someone else's failed **messianic** movement, faces the gallows as well. Somehow, through the cynicism, the casual local custom, the misunderstandings, the distortions, the plots and schemes and betrayals and denials, the Truth stands there in person, taking the death that would otherwise have fallen on the brigand.

Pilate didn't see it at the time. Even cunning Caiaphas probably didn't appreciate the irony of the point. But John wants us to see it. This is what the cross will mean. This is what truth is and does. Truth is what Jesus is; and Jesus is dying for Barabbas, and for Israel, and for the world.

And for you and me.

JOHN 19.1–7

Here's the Man!

[1]So Pilate then took Jesus and had him flogged. [2]The soldiers wove a crown of thorns, put it on his head, and dressed him up in a purple robe. [3]Then they came up to him and said, 'Hail, King of the Jews!' And they slapped him.

[4]Pilate went out again.

'Look,' he said to them, 'I'm bringing him out to you, so that you'll know I find no guilt in him.'

[5]So Jesus came out, wearing the crown of thorns and the purple cloak.

'Look!' said Pilate. 'Here's the man!'

[6]So when the chief priests and their attendants saw him, they gave a great shout.

'Crucify him!' they yelled. 'Crucify him!'

'Take him yourselves and crucify him!' said Pilate. 'I find him not guilty!'

[7]'We've got a law,' replied the Judaeans, 'and according to that law he deserves to die! He made himself the son of God!'

If you go into the Ashmolean museum in Oxford, you will see many treasures and beautiful objects from countries far away and centuries long past. But the last time I went in I was particularly struck by one set of objects. They weren't particularly beautiful or unique. But they told a story I hadn't seen in that way before.

These objects are statues. The main hall of the museum is lined with them. They are statues of Roman emperors and their families. Nothing unusual in that. They are, of course, interesting to the ancient historian, but most people looking at them would simply think, 'So: that's what Tiberius (or Gaius, or whoever) looked like.'

But I was struck by where these statues had been found, before they were brought to Oxford. They were from all over the Roman empire – except for Rome itself. The emperor and his family, after all, lived in Rome. There was less need for statues there (though they had a few, of course). But out in the provinces – in Gaul (modern France), Greece, Asia Minor (modern Turkey), Egypt and several other places – they put up statues. Larger-than-life images of the emperor and his immediate family.

Why?

They put these statues up *to show the local people who their rulers were*. The Romans weren't the first or the last to do it. They set up likenesses, images of themselves, so that the local people could look at them and say to themselves: that's the man who rules over us. That's the man we owe allegiance to. That's the man who has brought peace and justice to the world.

(And perhaps they might add, under their breath, That's the man we are paying such high taxes to! That's the man whose army killed all our fighting men! That's the man we'd like to get rid of!)

The idea of someone putting an image of themselves in the

country they rule is an important clue to understanding the very first chapter of the Bible. In Genesis, chapter 1, God creates the **heavens** and the earth. He makes the sea, the dry land, the plants, the fish, the birds and the animals. This is his world. This is the world over which he now rules. This is the world he wants to respond to him in love and gratitude.

So God places, within this new world, an image, a statue of himself. Except, of course, because of who God is, it isn't a statue made of stone or wood. It is itself a living being, like the animals but also unlike. This image is there for a purpose: so that, through this image, God can rule over his new world wisely and lovingly. And also that, in coming under the rule of this image, the creation can properly honour him, its creator.

This image, of course, is the human race (Genesis 1.26–28). In the image of God he made them; male and female he created them. And God gave them instructions to be fruitful and multiply, and look after the garden and the animals. Within the six-day creation of Genesis 1, the human race is created on the sixth day, the Friday. After that, God rests. The work is complete.

The writers of the Old Testament knew that this picture of the human being, ruling God's world under his lordship, revealing and exercising God's wise stewardship over creation, was quite like their picture of the ideal king. Indeed, sometimes it's hard to tell, when we read writings like Psalm 8, whether they are thinking of the whole human race or the king or both. And in some of the 'wisdom' writings of the Old Testament, and in later Judaism, the same coming together happens. Wisdom is what you need to be a truly human being; but it's the king, with Solomon as the best example, who is the truly wise person.

When we looked at the opening of John's **gospel**, we saw that the long and carefully crafted Prologue, telling the story of creation and new creation, was designed to lead the eye up to verse 14. This is the equivalent, within John 1, of Genesis 1.26–28. 'The **Word** became flesh, and lived among us.' The one who was with God, the one who *was* God, alongside the father and reflecting his character and love, became a human being. It was the most utterly appropriate thing that could have happened. It was like the sixth day of creation, only more so.

Now at last, with Roman emperors and creation stories in our heads, we find ourselves on a Friday morning, on the sixth day of the week, looking at the Roman governor and his peculiar new prisoner. He lets the soldiers dress him up as a king – of sorts: the crown of thorns, and the slapping about the face, tell you what they thought of such a claim. And Pilate says the words that still haunt us: 'Look! Here's the man!'

Here's the man! Here is the true image of the true God. Here is the one who has brought God's wisdom into the world. Here is the living embodiment of God, the one who has made the invisible God visible. Here is the king. Here is the breathing statue of the emperor-of-all, placed within the emperor's world so that people could see who was their true master. And all his rebel subjects can do is mock, and slap, and scream for his blood. He's made himself God's son, they say!

Well, John's reader knows by now that Jesus has indeed behaved as the one who, as of right, reflects God into the world. His own intimate knowledge of the father, and his sharing of that with his friends, is either a pack of lies or it's true. But – and here is the new thing, the thing not mentioned in Genesis 1 – this, too, this misrepresentation, these accusations, this crown of thorns (the sharp bits of creation, we note, drawing blood from creation's Lord), and the rest: all this is part of what it means to be God's image, planted in territory which belongs to God but which is in rebellion against him. 'He was in the world.' Now we have learned what John means by 'the world', that little sentence says it all.

It says, in particular, that when the living, loving God comes in person, in the person of his own son, to live among us rebels, in the world he made and still loves, the appropriate form for him to take is not the super-hero, sweeping through the rebel state with horses and chariots, defeating the rebellion in a blaze of glory. The appropriate form for him to take – the kind of living statue which will tell his subjects who he is, granted their wickedness – is the form Jesus has now taken. The king of the Jews, crowned with thorns. The innocent king, the true man, the one who told the truth and was accused of blasphemy. 'Here's the man!'

The words hang over the whole of chapter 19 as Jesus goes to the cross. This, John is telling us, is the true reflection of God. This is what it means that Jesus, the eternal **Word**, took our flesh. Look at this man, and you'll see your living, loving, bruised and bleeding God.

JOHN 19.8–16a

No King but Caesar

[8]When Pilate heard that, he was all the more afraid. [9]He went back into the residence and spoke to Jesus.

'Where do you come from?' he asked.

But Jesus gave him no answer.

[10]So Pilate addressed him again.

'Aren't you going to speak to me?' he said. 'Don't you know that I have the authority to let you go, and the authority to crucify you?'

[11]'You couldn't have any authority at all over me', replied Jesus, 'unless it was given to you from above. That's why the person who handed me over to you is guilty of a greater sin.'

[12]From that moment on, Pilate tried to let him go.

But the Judaeans shouted at him.

'If you let this fellow go,' they said, 'you are no friend of Caesar! Everyone who sets himself up as a king is speaking against Caesar!'

¹³So when Pilate heard them saying that, he brought Jesus out and sat down at the official judgment seat, called The Pavement (in Hebrew, 'Gabbatha'). ¹⁴It was the Preparation day of the Passover, and it was about midday.

'Look,' said Pilate, 'here is your king!'

¹⁵'Take him away!' they shouted. 'Take him away! Crucify him!'

'Do you want me to crucify your king?' asked Pilate.

'We have no king', the chief priests replied, 'except Caesar!'

¹⁶Then he handed him over to them to be crucified.

From our seats, high in the stands, we watched as the football match swung this way and that. Our team was doing well and scored a couple of early goals. We were delighted; surely they could hang on to a lead like that? When the opposition scored one back, with only ten minutes to go, we didn't mind too much. We were still in front, with not long to go.

But then the opposition brought on a substitute, fresh and lively. He was exactly what the other side needed. He put fresh heart into their whole team. We watched, helpless, as our side struggled to cope with the new challenge. The inevitable happened. First an equalizing goal. Then, three minutes before the end, the match-winner. We trudged off home, thinking of that moment when the whole game had swung away from us.

That is the feeling we get at verse 12 in this passage. Pilate is in charge. He's the governor. His word is law. He can kill people if he wants to; he can let them go if he wants to. He could order the troops to kill the chief **priests** themselves, if he thought he could get away with it. And when he decides that he really does want to let Jesus go, we assume he is going to be able to do it.

But the one constraint on Pilate is what people think of him back in Rome. Roman governors down the years were regularly prosecuted for maladministration. Provinces and cities would take their case to Rome, insisting on justice against the man who had been ruling them in Rome's name. There were famous instances of ex-governors paying heavy penalties. Under the empire, if the emperor decided someone was a nuisance, or surplus to requirements, he was quite capable of sending a message advising the man to commit suicide, to save his soldiers the bother of killing him themselves.

The threat of what Caesar might think is the secret weapon the chief priests have been keeping up their sleeves all this time. They didn't know whether they would have to use it, but when they realize that Pilate is wavering, and then has decided to let Jesus go, they bring it out. And from that moment Pilate is lost. What will people in Rome think? He can hear the sneers. 'You mean you had a man in front of you on a charge of making himself a rebel king – and you let him go? What sort of a governor are you? Don't you know you are supposed to be looking after Rome's interests? What's Caesar going to think of all this?'

Pilate had been afraid when he heard the chief priests say that Jesus had 'made himself the **son of God**' (verse 7). He was even more afraid when they pulled out this trump card. From here on he has lost the argument. But, on the way, we discover something more about the nature of his authority. Jesus, who remains silent about himself at this point, is still prepared to explain to Pilate how God's providence works! And we also discover, more darkly, something extraordinary about the position into which the chief priests have backed themselves.

Jesus doesn't challenge the authority that Pilate has over him. He merely informs him that it comes from above, from God. Like many Old Testament writers, Jesus accepts that even pagan states and empires hold their rule under the ultimate authority of the one true God. That isn't to say that God, or his true followers, need to approve of everything they do; only that the God who 'turns human wrath to his praise' (Psalm 76.10) takes the energy and organization of even wicked peoples, and makes it bring at least some measure of order to his world. Perhaps that is partly why Paul could say what he did in Romans 13.1–7. If Jesus could acknowledge even Pilate's authority, clearly a Christian view of secular power has to make room for some light and shade in its picture, and not construct too quickly an easy, black-and-white scheme in which some rulers are good and most simply bad.

Jesus warns Pilate that, though he holds delegated authority, this doesn't mean that there isn't real evil afoot. But this is a million miles from the view that the chief priests have painted themselves into. The real sting in this passage comes at the end. In order to reject the claim of Jesus to be the true reflection of their one true God, they find themselves driven back into the arms of pagan empire. 'We have no king but Caesar!'

It's a devastating thing to hear, coming from the lips of the official representatives of Judaism. The scriptures, songs and revolutionary slogans of Judaism had spoken for a thousand years of its God as the true king, of the coming **Messiah** as God's true king, and of pagan rulers as a sham, a pretence, a bunch of trumped-up idolaters. What would Isaiah have said to the chief priests? How would they feel, next time they heard the psalms sung in the **Temple**? What would they say to the crowds, many of whom had supported Jesus precisely because they hoped he would be the king who would free them from Caesar?

These questions haven't gone away. They still float in the air in our puzzled world. Who is the world's true lord? What authority have governments, and how does that relate to the authority of God? Sometimes, when people don't want Jesus as Lord, they find themselves driven, like the chief priests, into some form of pagan empire.

Pagan empire comes in various forms. It may appear as the totalitarianism which claims divinity, and hence absolute allegiance, for itself. Or it may appear as the liberal democracy which banishes 'God' from its system altogether, and then regards itself as free to carve up the world to its own advantage without moral restraint. Either way, the choice becomes stark. Are we with Pilate – nervously allowing himself to be manoeuvred into dangerous compromise? Are we with the chief priests – pressing home a political advantage without realizing that we are pushing ourselves backwards towards complete capitulation? Or are we with Jesus – silent in the middle, continuing to reflect the love of God into his muddled and tragic world?

JOHN 19.16b–24

The King of the Jews

[16b]So they took Jesus away. [17]He carried his own cross, and went to the spot called 'Skull Place' (in Hebrew, 'Golgotha'). [18]That was where they crucified him. They also crucified two others, one on either side of him, with Jesus in the middle.

[19]Pilate wrote a notice and had it placed on the cross. The notice said:

JESUS OF NAZARETH THE KING OF THE JEWS

[20]Lots of the Judaeans read this notice, because the place where Jesus was crucified was close to the city. It was written in Hebrew, Latin and Greek.

[21]So the chief priests said to Pilate, 'Don't write "The King of the Jews"! Write that he *said* "I am the King of the Jews"!'

[22]'What I've written,' replied Pilate, 'I've written.'

[23]When the soldiers had crucified Jesus, they took his clothes and divided them into four parts, giving each soldier one part. When they came to his tunic, they found that it was a single piece of cloth, woven from top to bottom.

[24]'Let's not tear it,' they said to each other. 'Let's throw lots for it, to see who's going to have it.'

This was so that the Bible would be fulfilled, when it says,

> They took my clothes and divided them up,
> They threw the dice to decide on my garments.

And that's what the soldiers did.

There was a shocking photograph in the newspaper the other day. A cart was being driven through the streets of a city in the Far East. On the cart were standing fifteen or twenty men. Round the neck of each, hanging from a string, was a notice. On the notice was written the particular crime they were accused of.

When they reached the end of their journey, so the report said, they were taken off the cart. Two of the men were selected, and were publicly beheaded. The others were taken back to prison, to await the pleasure of the government.

The purpose of the notices was obvious. They were to rub in the point to the people who were watching (and there were plenty of people watching): that's what will happen if you get up to this sort of thing. The 'sort of thing' in question was actions or teachings which the government interpreted as being revolutionary.

The Romans used more or less exactly the same system. That's what's going on when Pilate places a notice above Jesus' head on the cross. Sometimes condemned Roman prisoners, like the ones in the newspaper, carried the notice around their neck on the way to the place of execution, so that all the more people could see, and take warning.

The notice itself is full of irony. The chief **priests** are furious with Pilate. He doesn't believe Jesus is the King of the Jews any more than they do, and they don't want him making fun of them in this way. Pilate, of course, is getting his own back. It's a calculated snub.

'You wanted him crucified, didn't you?' we can feel him thinking. 'Well, I've done it. And I reserve the right to say what

I want on the public notice. As far as I'm concerned, he really is "The King of the Jews" – the only sort of king you crazy people deserve! This is what I've done to him, and this is what I'd be happy to do to the whole lot of you!'

Once again we must listen to what John is telling us, as Jesus goes to his death. Remember how Caiaphas had said more than he had known when he spoke, callously, about one man dying for the people (11.49–50). Remember how Jesus had been approached by some Greeks, and how in his comment on their request he had said that when he was 'lifted up from the earth' he would 'draw all people to himself' (12.32). Remember how Peter had declared that *he* would lay down his life for *Jesus*, and how Jesus had gently questioned whether he'd got that idea the right way round (13.37–38). Bring all that together, stand at the foot of the cross and look up at the notice that Pilate has written. What do you see?

You see, to begin with, that it's written in the three major languages of the time and place: Hebrew, Latin and Greek. You could get a long way with those languages. Wherever you are in the world in our own day, if you can speak English, Chinese and a major local language, you'll probably be able to understand the public notices. In Jesus' world, Hebrew (John probably means Aramaic) was the local language. In the wider world, Greek was almost universal, like English in much of today's world. Latin was the official language of the empire.

But what John is telling us, of course, is that Jesus is now announced as Israel's **Messiah** to all the world. This is what he had said would happen. The world doesn't at the moment know that what it needs, to rescue it from its desperate plight, is the Messiah promised by the one God to Israel. But this is what John believed. Israel's Messiah, after all, will rule from sea to sea, from one end of the world to the other. All nations will do him homage (Psalm 72).

But how can this happen, if the Messiah is being executed

as a common criminal, or a revolutionary? John's answer is unambiguous; it is precisely *through* his execution that it will now happen. As the King, he is also fulfilling the extraordinary biblical prophecies about the suffering righteous one, in whom the sufferings of Israel would come to their height, and through whose tribulation and death evil would be exhausted and the **kingdom of God** be born on earth.

One of the most popular of these biblical prophecies among the early Christians was Psalm 22. That is the psalm from which, according to Matthew (27.46) and Mark (15.34), Jesus himself quoted, or perhaps we should say screamed out, at the moment of his greatest agony: 'My God, my God, why did you abandon me?' As that psalm continues its awful litany of suffering, one of the many horrors it describes is the moment when the sufferer is not only stripped naked but suffers the added indignity of seeing people gambling for his clothes.

John doesn't need to do more than give the briefest description of the gambling at the foot of the cross, and to draw our attention to the psalm in question. He leaves us to think through the implication. Jesus is the fulfilment of prophecy and sacred song. He is the righteous sufferer. He is the true King. He is the one through whose shameful death the weight of Israel's sin, and behind that the sin of the whole world, is being dealt with. The King of the Jews is God's chosen representative, not merely to rule the world but to redeem it.

JOHN 19.25–30

The Death of Jesus

[25]Jesus' mother was standing beside his cross. So was her sister, Mary the wife of Clopas, with Mary Magdalene too. [26]Jesus saw his mother, and the disciple he specially loved, standing there.

'Mother,' he said. 'Look! there's your son.'

²⁷Then he spoke to the disciple.

'Look!' he said. 'There's your mother.'

From that time, the disciple welcomed her into his own home.

²⁸After this, Jesus knew that everything had been completed. 'I'm thirsty,' he said (fulfilling what the Bible had said).

²⁹There was a jar there full of sour wine. So they put a sponge filled with the sour wine on a hyssop rod and lifted it to his mouth. ³⁰Jesus drank it.

'It's all done!' he said.

Then he let his head drop, and gave up his spirit.

A colleague of mine worked in Lebanon during the awful civil war in the second half of the twentieth century. He reported an interesting phenomenon, which helps us to understand what was happening at the foot of the cross.

Rival militias were stalking the streets of Beirut. Men, armed to the teeth, were struggling for control of different streets and key buildings. No man dared venture out of doors unless he was heavily armed, preferably in a group or with some kind of protection.

But the women were free to come and go as they pleased. It was understood that they wouldn't be combatants; and also, one assumes, that they would need to do basic shopping, to keep families going even amid such civil unrest. A man was vulnerable to being attacked, kidnapped or killed. A woman was not.

This sheds light, incidentally, on the status of women in the early church. Acts 8.3 reports that women as well as men were the victims of persecution. Clearly they were perceived as a threat, just like the men. But at the time of Jesus' death this wasn't so. The **disciples** had all run away to hide. They didn't dare show their faces. But there was no problem about the women revealing by their actions that they were part of Jesus' entourage. Nobody was going to bother arresting them.

So why didn't they arrest 'the disciple Jesus specially loved'? How did he manage to be there?

As with 18.15–16, I think the answer must be that he was still very young. He was just a lad. The soldiers wouldn't regard him as a serious potential revolutionary. He wasn't about to rally the others, to choose a new leader and carry on the **kingdom**-movement that had now come to a sorry end. He may not yet have turned twenty. He probably hadn't yet grown a beard. He didn't look a threat.

The moving scene that follows between him, Jesus' mother and Jesus himself has been the subject of much painting and meditation. Many churches have Mary and John (let's call him 'John' for the sake of discussion, though we may never know for certain that it was him) painted at the foot of the cross, on either side. I once worked in a church where, behind the altar, there was a large stained-glass window portraying the crucifixion, with Mary on the left and John on the right. I often used to draw attention to it when preaching at weddings: the man and the woman meet at the foot of the cross.

But this moment – the last time we meet Jesus' mother in the **gospel** story – is full of pathos all of its own. Think back to that story, early on in the gospel, when Mary pointed out to Jesus that the wine had run out (2.3–4). She didn't understand, then, that his time hadn't yet come, but she knew that the way to get things done was for people to do whatever he said. She doesn't understand, now, that his time has come at last; that this was where it was all leading; that his calling, to turn the water of human **life** into the rich wine of God's love, was now at last being fulfilled. We assume that she quickly came to believe all this through Jesus' **resurrection**; and we assume it the more readily because of what happens here. John takes her to his own home and welcomes her as though she were his own mother.

But the story of the water and the wine has more resonance

with this scene than simply Jesus' comment to Mary. Here is Jesus, thirsty; and they give him the low-grade sour wine that the soldiers used. He gave others the best wine, so good that people remarked on it. He himself, at his moment of agony, has the cheap stuff that the lower ranks in the army drank when on duty.

With that, two other windows open up for us, shafts of light that John allows to fall on the simple and sad story of Jesus' death.

First, we are reminded of the many times when Jesus has spoken of water. There is the 'sign' of chapter 2, which we just mentioned. There is the long discussion about 'living water' with the woman of Samaria, in chapter 4. Jesus offered her that 'living water', and it was clear that he had it in abundant supply. Then, in chapter 6, he spoke of those who believed in him not only never being hungry, but also never being thirsty. He amplified this in chapter 7, speaking exuberantly of the 'living water' that was available for anyone who came to him. They could satisfy their thirst for ever by believing in him. Indeed, they would have 'rivers of living water' springing up from within themselves.

All this only heightens our sense of horror and awe, as we get the full impact of what John is saying, at the thought of Jesus himself being . . . thirsty. Had the water of life failed? Had the wine run out for good? He saved others; could he not save himself? As with the crown of thorns and the mocking purple robe, this (John is saying) is part of the truth of it all. This is how Jesus must do what only he can do. He must come to the place where everyone else is, the place of thirst, shame and death. That, too, is a fulfilment of scripture (Psalm 69.21). That is his glory and, yes, his joy.

But there is one more thing that John wants to say, and the allusion to chapter 2 reminds us of this as well.

The changing of water to wine was, as he told us clearly, the first in the sequence of 'signs' by which Jesus revealed his glory. The second was the healing of the nobleman's son at Capernaum (4.46–54). From then on he leaves us to count up the 'signs', and different readers have reckoned them differently. I think the most convincing sequence goes like this. The third 'sign' is the healing of the paralysed man at the pool (5.1–9). The fourth is the multiplication of loaves and fishes (6.1–14). The fifth is the healing of the man born blind (9.1–12). And the sixth is the raising of Lazarus (11.1–44).

John cannot have intended the sequence to stop at six. With Genesis 1 in the back of his mind from the very start, the sequence of seven signs, completing the accomplishment of the new creation, has an inevitability about it. Now here we are, at the foot of the cross. John has told us throughout his gospel that when Jesus is 'lifted up', this will be the moment of God's glory shining through him in full strength. And the 'signs' are the things that reveal God's glory. I regard it as more or less certain that he intends the crucifixion itself to function as the seventh 'sign'.

As though to confirm this, Jesus gives one last cry. 'It's finished!' 'It's all done!' 'It's complete!' He has finished the work that the father had given him to do (17.4). He has loved 'to the very end' his own who were in the world (13.1). He has accomplished the full and final task.

The word that I've translated 'It's all done!' is actually a single word in the original language. It's the word that people would write on a bill after it had been paid. The bill is dealt with. It's finished. The price has been paid. Yes, says John: and Jesus' work is now complete, in that sense as in every other. It is upon this finished, complete work that his people from that day to this can stake their lives.

JOHN 19.31–37

Blood and Water

³¹It was the day of Preparation. The coming sabbath was a very special one, and the Judaeans were anxious that the bodies should not remain on the cross during it. So they asked Pilate to have the legs of the crucified men broken, and their bodies taken away.

³²So the soldiers came and broke the legs of the men who were crucified with Jesus, first the one, then the other. ³³But when they came to Jesus, they saw that he was already dead, so they didn't break his legs. ³⁴Instead, one of the soldiers thrust a spear into his side, and blood and water came out. ³⁵(The one who saw it is giving evidence, and his evidence is true! He knows he's speaking the truth, so that you may believe!) ³⁶These things, you see, came about so that the Bible might come true: 'No bone of his will be broken.' ³⁷And, again, another passage in the Bible says, 'They shall look on the one whom they pierced.'

He came up at the end of the service and shook me warmly by the hand. 'I didn't really know why I was coming here this morning,' he said. 'I wouldn't normally have made the effort. I'd have gone somewhere closer to home. But something made me come. And then when you said what you did in your sermon' (he mentioned something I'd said which, unknown to me, was exactly what he'd needed to help him forwards at a particular point), 'I knew why I was here.'

Many preachers will have had that experience. And many of us, too, know the moment when a strange compulsion makes us go to a place where, though we couldn't have known it, someone we needed to see was waiting. It's only when you look back, sometimes over a long period, that you notice these patterns and realize that, despite the horrors and tragedies of life, God is quietly working his purposes out.

The young man at the foot of the cross must have asked himself a thousand times why it had to happen. He must have asked himself many times why he had to be there. Why couldn't he have stayed in hiding like the others? Why did he have to see this horror? But within a few days he knew. And finally, as he turned it all over and over in his mind after a lifetime of praying and teaching, he could see the pattern and leave his own mark on the story at this point. He knew why he had needed to be there.

He needed to be there because people would say, before too long, that Jesus hadn't really died on the cross. The story of the **resurrection** is so huge, so mind-blowing, that it doesn't fit into anybody's preconceived world-view. Of course it doesn't. Nobody, no society, no individual, has by nature a way of looking at the world which allows easily for someone to be crucified on a Friday, thoroughly dead and buried, and then alive again on the Sunday with a **life** which death itself cannot touch. So some, confronted by the news, will say he stayed dead. It was just his **spirit**; a vision, a ghost, a hallucination. Others will say he never really died. He just swooned. He fainted. They took him down quickly and he revived in the tomb. This was beginning to be said by many sceptics – and perhaps also by some people within the church – at the time John's **gospel** was being written.

Now there are all sorts of good reasons for rejecting both these accounts. That is another topic for another place. But the writer of this gospel has the best possible answer to the suggestion that Jesus didn't really die. He was there; he saw it; he is giving first-hand evidence.

What did he see, and why? To understand this, you need to understand, first, why the Judaeans wanted the bodies off the cross; second, how the Roman soldiers went about their job; and third, what happens, medically, inside a recently dead body.

The Judaeans wanted the bodies taking down because it was Passover-time. The next day was not just a **sabbath**, but a very special one in their calendar. The Bible had insisted that bodies of executed people should not be left hanging there overnight (Deuteronomy 21.23); it would pollute the land. So they asked Pilate to have them taken down.

Pilate, of course, hadn't had the men crucified in order to let them go half dead. Crucified people often remained alive, or half alive, for some days; Jesus was unusual in that, after his long ordeal, he had died within a few hours. The way crucifixion killed people was a form of torture. Suspended by the arms, you wouldn't be able to breathe; so you would push yourself up with your legs in order to take a breath. People would go on doing this until they ran out of strength, and then they would suffocate. So the quick, and typically brutal, way to finish it off (my history teacher used to say that if there was a nasty way of doing something, the Romans probably did it that way) was to break the legs. Suffocation would then follow quickly.

That's what they did to the other two. The crack of a spear-butt on human bone; a half-scream of agony; convulsions; then silence. But when they came to Jesus, he was already dead. The soldiers were puzzled. That was quick! Was he, perhaps, just faking? No Roman soldier would let a condemned criminal escape death. His own life would be forfeit if he did. So, just to be sure, he stuck his spear hard up into Jesus' ribs; either it would kill him, or it would prove he was already dead.

The test was negative. After death, the body fluids separate out. The medical details have been interpreted in different ways, and we don't know whether the spear might not have pierced Jesus' heart. (John doesn't tell us which side it was, though artists have normally painted the wound in Jesus' right side.) The point seems to be, though, that whereas a living body would have produced blood, a dead body, from somewhere in the chest or stomach, would produce a mixture of clotting blood and a watery substance. Jesus really was dead. The writer saw it, and insists on the truth of his evidence.

But of course, at this moment of all moments, none of this is simply told for the sake of historical detail, vital though that is (the **Word** really did become *flesh*, not a phantom!). John has left us in no doubt that all these details, too, though from one point of view 'accidental' (nobody could have guessed what the soldiers might do next), were all to be seen as **heaven**-sent signs of what it all meant. We only have to think back through the gospel, to all the occasions where water or blood are mentioned, to realize that again and again they point to Jesus as the source of life, cleansing and purification. All these themes come together at this moment.

And, in particular, they all point to Jesus as the true Passover lamb. At the moment when the lambs are being killed in the **Temple** (John is careful to tell us that it was Passover that day; this creates a puzzle when we put his book together with the others, but that is another story), Jesus himself is the true Passover lamb, who takes away the sin of the world. The Passover regulations specified that no bone of the lamb should be broken (Exodus 12.46; Numbers 9.12).

At the same time – here, as so often in John, two themes are combined – Jesus dies as the true **Messiah**, bearing the sorrow and shame of Israel and hence of the world. 'They shall look on the one whom they pierced'; this is a quotation from Zechariah 12.10, a passage which speaks, darkly to our minds but powerfully in Jesus' day, about the time of great suffering and mourning which will come upon Jerusalem, through which God will bring about redemption, rescue, deliverance. The immediate result of the piercing and mourning, according to the prophet, is that a fountain will be opened for the house of David and the people of Jerusalem, a fountain which will cleanse them from sin and impurity (Zechariah 13.1).

John would have agreed. That is what the water and the blood mean. A real death, bringing real deliverance from sin.

JOHN 19.38–42

The Burial of Jesus

[38]After this, Joseph of Arimathea asked Pilate if he could take Jesus' body away. He was a disciple of Jesus, but he kept it secret because he was afraid of the Judaeans. Pilate gave him permission. So he came and took his body. [39]Nicodemus came too (the man who, at first, had visited Jesus by night). He brought a concoction of myrrh and aloes, about a hundred pounds in weight. [40]They took Jesus' body, and wrapped it up in cloths with the spices, according to the normal Judaean burial custom.

[41]There was a garden in the place where he was crucified. In the garden, there was a new tomb where nobody had ever been buried. [42]So, because the tomb was nearby, and because of the Judaean day of Preparation, they buried Jesus there.

The camel was called Michael.

He stood, with his owner, outside the walls of Jerusalem. Our day's tour was over, and one member of the party at least was keen to do something different. I went with her to speak to the camel's owner, one of the many Arabs who eke out a living as best they can in that spot. Before we knew what was happening he had half lifted, half pushed both of us onto the camel's back. Then he tapped the camel on its shoulder and shouted 'Hallelujah!'

The camel stood up (looking back at one point with a puzzled expression to see why his load was so heavy), and the owner led him forward along the street. Every few paces he shouted 'Hallelujah!' again. (It wasn't exactly what we wanted to shout, wobbling precariously and swaying from side to side.) We got to the end, turned round, and came back to where we'd started. With a final 'Hallelujah!' the camel knelt down, and we climbed off.

'Why do you shout "Hallelujah!" all the time?' I asked the owner as I paid him for our ride.

He put his mouth close to my ear.

'Because I am a lover of Jesus,' he replied, softly.

Suddenly I was back in the first century. '*But secretly, for fear of the Judaeans.*' Fear of his own kin, in that militant and much-battled place. Fear of Muslim hostility, and perhaps of Jewish anger too. A warmth of recognition swept over me. I squeezed his hand, adding some more shekels. His camel and his Hallelujahs. They were what he could do for Jesus, there outside the walls of Jerusalem.

Joseph and Nicodemus brought what they could, too, outside those same walls. A hundred pounds of spices (in our weight-system, about eighty pounds): a hundred times the amount that Mary had poured over Jesus in Bethany (12.3), and that had caused people to grumble at the extravagance. It was the kind of quantity (and quality, for that matter) that you might use for a king. That was probably the point. Joseph and Nicodemus agreed with Pilate's notice, though for very different reasons. If Israel ever had a king, surely this was the man.

We haven't met Joseph before in this **gospel**. According to the other accounts, he owned the tomb; John makes it sound as though it just happened to be close by and available. The point he stresses, though, is that it had never been used before; verse 41 is very emphatic on the point. John is already looking ahead to what people will think when he tells them the next part of his story: supposing there was some mistake, supposing they got the tombs muddled, supposing . . .

No. It was a brand new tomb. There could be no mistake.

We have met Nicodemus before (3.1–10; 7.50–52), as John reminds us. His night-time visit to the strange new teacher was the first of the great extended dialogues that Jesus had with people throughout this gospel. It was in response to him that Jesus explained about the new birth, being born from water and the **spirit**. It was in developing that idea that he spoke of Moses lifting up the serpent in the wilderness, and the **son of man** being lifted up in the same way, so that everyone who believes in him will have **eternal life** (3.14–16). After that he spoke of people who do evil hating the light, and not wanting to come into the light, while people who do what is right come to the light, so that it may be clearly seen that what they have done has been done 'in God' (3.19–21).

So here is Nicodemus, coming this time just before nightfall. This time he is in the light, albeit only just; the body must be buried before nightfall, when the **sabbath** begins. He has come into the light. His discipleship may have taken a while to develop, through the time when he stood up for Jesus on a point of **law** and was mocked for his pains (7.50–52), to this moment when, with nothing to gain and everything to lose, he performs the last service he can for his strange dead king.

The burial customs of that time and place, as we saw in chapter 11 at the tomb of Lazarus, were quite different from most of our modern ones. No coffins; no cremations. The tomb would be a cave hollowed out in the rock; archaeologists have found lots of them. The cave would be big enough inside for two or more people to walk in, though the doorway would probably be quite small, about four feet high. Then there would be ledges on either side.

When you created a tomb like that, it was a lot of work, and you would want to be able to use it several times. The first body you put in would be laid on one of the ledges. It was quite likely that you would want to bury a second body before the first one had finished decomposing; that was one reason for wrapping the body in strips of cloth along with a large amount of spices and perfumes. In between burials, the tomb would be secured against grave-robbers by a large, heavy circular stone that would roll in a groove in front of the door.

When decomposition was complete, the bones would be collected and placed into a bone-box (an 'ossuary'). The bone-box would then be stored either at the back of the cave or in some other safe location. The burial thus took place in two stages, not one as in most burials today. Months, perhaps even a year or more, might intervene between the one and the other.

John, we may be sure, intends us to remember the last time we stood before a tomb. Jesus wept outside Lazarus's tomb (11.35), but when they rolled the stone away there was no smell of decomposition (11.41). Wait, John says to us. Watch with me through this sabbath, this quiet, sad rest. Wait for this, the final day, the seventh day, to pass. God rested on the seventh day. So must Jesus. But this whole book has been about new creation. Wait for the eighth day.

JOHN 20.1–10

The Empty Tomb

¹On the first day of the week, very early, Mary Magdalene came to the tomb while it was still dark.

She saw that the stone had been rolled away from the tomb. ²So she ran off, and went to Simon Peter, and to the other disciple, the one Jesus loved.

'They've taken the master out of the tomb!' she said. 'We don't know where they've put him!'

³So Peter and the other disciple set off and went to the tomb. ⁴Both of them ran together. The other disciple ran faster than Peter, and got to the tomb first. ⁵He stooped down and saw the linen cloths lying there, but he didn't go in. ⁶Then Simon Peter came up, following him, and went into the tomb. He saw the linen cloths lying there, ⁷and the napkin that had been around his head, not lying with the other cloths, but folded up in a place by itself.

⁸Then the other disciple, who had arrived first at the tomb, went into the tomb as well. He saw, and he believed. ⁹They did not yet know, you see, that the Bible had said he must rise again from the dead.

¹⁰Then the disciples returned to their homes.

Darkness on the face of the deep. The formless beginning, the chaos. The void. The beginning.

The wind and the word. God's breath, God's speech, summoning things never known before. Life and light. The first day. Creation.

In the beginning was the **Word** . . . and the Word became flesh. The flesh has spoken, breathed, brought life and light. New creation has spilled out around him wherever he has gone. 'Here's the man!' The sixth day. Creation is complete. God saw all he had made, and it was very good.

Flesh dies. Chaos comes again. Darkness descends on the little weeping group at the cross. Two men in the fading light do what has to be done. Then the long **sabbath**, the rest in the cold tomb.

And now, still in the darkness, the first day of the week. The new week. The new creation. The eighth day. Eyes red from weeping and sleepless sabbath nights. Women at the tomb; perhaps to bring more spices, perhaps just to weep, perhaps just to be there, because there was nowhere else to be, nothing else to do, nothing else that mattered, that would ever matter.

Mary Magdalene doesn't feature in John's **gospel** until her appearance, with the other Marys, at the foot of the cross. John has told us nothing of her history; the little we know, we know from the other gospels. But her place here is spectacular. She is the first **apostle**, the apostle to the apostles: the first to bring the news that the tomb was empty. And, in the next section, a greater privilege yet: the first to see, to meet, to speak with the risen master himself.

For the moment, the empty tomb is simply another twist of the knife. Chaos upon chaos. Someone's taken him away. No **faith**, no hope, no 'maybe, after all . . .'. Just a cruel trick. Some gardener, some labourer, some soldier, someone's servant. But we must find out. It's urgent. She runs back into the city, back to Peter in his hiding place, back to the young lad she had stood with by the cross, the one Jesus specially loved.

They run, too. (There is more running in these verses than in the rest of the gospels put together.) The younger man gets there first. Sure enough, the tomb is open and empty. And here's a curious thing: there are the linen cloths, lying there. Someone has not only taken the body away; they have first gone to the trouble of *unwrapping* it. Why on earth would you do that? Where has that happened before?

Peter, out of breath, arrives at the tomb a few moments later. He acts in character: no waiting, no beating about the bush, no shall-we-shan't-we. In he goes. And here's an even more curious thing: the linen cloths are lying there; but the single cloth, the napkin that had been around Jesus' head, isn't with the others. It's in a place by itself. Someone, having unwrapped the body (a complicated task in itself), has gone to the trouble of laying out the cloths to create an effect. It looks as though the body wasn't picked up and unwrapped, but had just disappeared, leaving the empty cloths, like a collapsed balloon when the air has gone out of it.

(The archaeologists have found at least one first-century tomb, just south of where Jesus' tomb must have been, with grave-cloths just like this, surrounding what's left of the bones. The body must have been buried just before the devastating Jewish–Roman war of AD 66–70, and the secondary burial of the bones never took place.)

Then comes the moment. The younger man, the beloved **disciple**, goes into the tomb after Peter. And the idea they had had to that point about what must have happened – someone taking the body away, but unwrapping it first – suddenly looks stupid and irrelevant. Something quite new surges up in the young disciple, a wild delight at God's creative power. He remembers the moment ever afterwards. A different sensation. A bit like falling in love; a bit like sunrise; a bit like the sound of rain at the end of a long drought.

A bit like faith. Oh, he'd had faith before. He had believed that Jesus was the **Messiah**. He had believed that God had sent him, that he was God's man for God's people and God's world. But this was different. 'He saw, *and believed.*' Believed that new creation had begun. Believed that the world had turned the corner, out of its long winter and into spring at last. Believed that God had said 'Yes' to Jesus, to all that he had been and done. Believed that Jesus was alive again.

Not 'believed that Jesus had gone to **heaven**'. People often still think that that's what Christians mean when they say he was raised from the dead. John is quite clear, later on in this passage, that that's not what he's talking about (verse 17). He is talking about **resurrection**.

Everybody in the ancient world knew that resurrection didn't happen. More: they knew it *couldn't* happen. They spoke of it, in the classical world of Greece and Rome, as something one might imagine but which never actually occurred, and never could or would. The Jews, though, began to believe that it would. Not all of them, mind; the **Sadducees** resolutely stuck out against it. And they weren't all clear exactly what it would mean, what it would be like. But they believed, as we saw in 11.24, that when resurrection happened it would happen to all God's people all at once. (Perhaps, even, to all people everywhere, as in 5.28–29.) Not – this is the point – to one person in the middle of time. That would be an odd, outlandish event, unimagined, unheard-of.

When Jesus raised Lazarus, Lazarus returned to the present **life**. He came back again. The echoes of the Lazarus story in the present one are there partly to tell us that it was the same kind of event, but mostly to tell us that it wasn't. Lazarus needed someone to untie him from his cloths, and the napkin round his head. Jesus left his behind altogether. Lazarus came back into a world where death threats still mattered (12.10). Jesus had gone on, through death and out into a new world, a new creation, a new life beyond, where death itself had been defeated and life, sheer life, life in all its fullness, could begin at last.

Ask people around the world what they think is the biggest day of the year for Christians. Most will say 'Christmas'. That's what our society has achieved: a romantic mid-winter festival (though we don't actually know what time of the year Jesus was born) from which most of the things that really matter (the danger, the politics) are carefully excluded. The true answer – and I wish the churches would find ways of making this clear – is Easter. This is the moment of new creation. If it hadn't been for Easter, nobody would ever have dreamed of celebrating Christmas. This is the first day of God's new week. The darkness has gone, and the sun is shining.

JOHN 20.11–18

Mary Magdalene and the Risen Jesus

[11]But Mary stood outside the tomb, crying. As she wept, she stooped down to look into the tomb. [12]There she saw two angels, clothed in white, one at the head and one at the feet of where Jesus' body had been lying.

[13]'Woman,' they said to her, 'why are you crying?'

'They've taken away my master,' she said, 'and I don't know where they've put him!'

[14]As she said this she turned round, and saw Jesus standing there. She didn't know it was Jesus.

[15]'Woman,' Jesus said to her, 'why are you crying? Who are you looking for?'

She guesssed he must be the gardener.

'Sir,' she said, 'if you've carried him off somewhere, tell me where you've put him, and I will take him away.'

[16]'Mary!' said Jesus.

She turned and spoke in Aramaic.

'Rabbouni!' she said (which means 'Teacher').

[17]'Don't cling to me,' said Jesus. 'I haven't yet gone up to the father. But go to my brothers and say to them, "I'm going up to my father and your father – to my God and your God."'

[18]Mary Magdalene went and told the disciples, 'I've seen the master!' and that he had said these things to her.

The first time I went to stay with a family in Germany, I learnt enough German before the trip to know the basic rules of politeness. When people say 'you' in German, there are two forms, like the old English 'ye' (for more than one person) and 'thou' (for just one). In Germany it is polite to call everybody you meet by the more-than-one word, 'Sie'. You only use the one-person word, 'Du', when talking to little children.

Until, that is, they tell you otherwise. The family I stayed with were delightful and very friendly. They made me extremely welcome, looked after me, and put up with my stumbling attempts to speak their language. I always called them 'Sie'. But it was only after several days that my host, at supper, made a quiet announcement. I had been with them for some while now, and we had got to know one another. It was now appropriate that I should call them 'Du'. This was a new stage of friendship and intimacy. The nearest we come to it in English is, I suppose, when someone who you have been calling 'Dr Smith' or 'Mr Jones' insists that instead you should call him or her by the name friends use, by their first name.

This passage gives us a moment like that. It's a moment when it becomes clear, to the careful reader of John's **gospel**, that something extraordinary has taken place, not only to Jesus – though that's extraordinary enough – but to the way the world is, the way God is, the way God and the **disciples** now are. Up to this point Jesus has spoken about God as 'the father', or 'the father who sent me', or 'my father'. He has called his followers 'disciples', 'servants' and 'friends'. Now all that has changed. Feel the force of verse 17: 'Go and say to *my brothers*, I am going up to my father *and your father*, to my God *and your God*.'

Something has altered, decisively. Something has been achieved. A new relationship has sprung to life like a sudden spring flower. The disciples are welcomed into a new world: a world where they can know God the way Jesus knew God, where they can be intimate children with their father.

They can be, in other words, true Israelites at last. Israel's calling was to be God's son, God's firstborn (Exodus 4.22). Israel struggled with that vocation. The idea survives in various Old Testament writings and in subsequent Jewish thought, but there was a sense that if Israel really was God's child an estrangement had taken place. When Jesus told the story of a son who went off in disgrace into a far country, his hearers knew what he was talking about (Luke 15.11–32). But now Jesus has broken through the **exile**, has made a way back from the ultimate far country, death itself. A way back to the father's house. And everyone who follows Jesus is welcome there in his name, as a beloved son or daughter.

This stunning invitation comes as Mary acts out one of the oldest dramas in the world. Stand with her as she weeps. Think of someone you know, or have seen on television or in the newspapers, who has cried bitterly this last week. Bring them too, and stand there with Mary. Don't rush it. Tears have their own natural rhythm. Hold them – the people, the tears – in your mind as you stand outside the tomb. And then, when the moment is right, stoop down and look into the tomb itself. Be prepared for a surprise.

Where had the angels come from? They hadn't been there a

few moments before, when Peter and John had been inside the tomb. Or maybe they had been. Maybe sometimes you can only see angels through tears. Whatever. When people are afraid, angels tend to tell them not to be. When people are in tears, angels ask why. Say it out loud. Whoever you've brought with you to stand here, listen to them say it too. They have taken away . . . my home, my husband, my children, my rights, my dignity, my hopes, my life. They have taken away my master. The world's grief, Israel's grief, concentrated in Mary's grief.

Now, as you stand with Mary and ponder her answer, and the answers the question would receive today from around the world, turn around and see the strange figure who's standing there. Who is he? What's he doing? Who do you think he is?

Mary's intuitive guess, that he must be the gardener, was wrong at one level and right, deeply right, at another. This is the new creation. Jesus is the beginning of it. Remember Pilate: 'Here's the man!' Here he is: the new Adam, the gardener, charged with bringing the chaos of God's creation into new order, into flower, into fruitfulness. He has come to uproot the thorns and thistles and replace them with blossoms and harvests. As we stand there and listen, overhearing Mary's conversation (a typical sequence, for John, of people getting the wrong idea), let the pain of the people you're with speak itself to Jesus, whether or not they know who he is.

Then listen for the name. It is greeting, consolation, gentle rebuke ('Come on! Don't you know me?') and invitation, all rolled into one. Of course we know him. Of course we don't know him. He is the same. He is different. He is alive, with a new sort of life, the like of which we'd never seen before. Let Jesus call your own name, and the name of whoever you've brought with you, whoever needs his love and healing today. And then take it from there. Let the prayer flow on into whatever new conversation is appropriate.

The most puzzling feature of the passage is Jesus' warning to Mary in verse 17. 'Don't cling to me'; or, as some translations say, 'Don't touch me.' Two magnificent and world-famous paintings, by Titian and Rembrandt, explore, but don't capture, the poignant scene. What did Jesus mean?

Some have thought that his **resurrection** body was so new, so different, that he didn't want Mary trying to touch him and getting the wrong idea, thinking he was a ghost. That seems hardly likely in view of the other accounts, and the subsequent invitation to Thomas to touch and see (though admittedly that was a week later). I think it's more likely that it was a warning to Mary that the new relationship with him was not going to be like the old one. He wouldn't be going around Galilee and Judaea any more, walking the lanes with them, sharing regular meals, discussing, talking, praying. They would see him now and then, but soon it would be time for him to 'go to the father', as he had said over and over in chapters 14—17. That's why I think 'Don't cling to me' is the best way of saying what he said here. 'Don't try to keep me, to possess me.' Strange words for a strange moment.

Mary is not upset by this. She doesn't feel it as a rebuff. She has business in hand. Once again she is the **apostle** to the apostles. 'I've seen the master, and this is what he said!' Nothing like fresh, first-hand evidence.

And it still counts today. If someone in the first century had wanted to invent a story about people seeing Jesus, they wouldn't have dreamed of giving the star part to a woman. Let alone Mary Magdalene.

JOHN 20.19–23

Jesus and the Disciples

[19]On the evening of that day, the first day of the week, the doors were shut where the disciples were, for fear of the

Judaeans. Jesus came and stood in the middle of them.

'Peace be with you,' he said.

[20]With these words, he showed them his hands and his side. Then the disciples were overjoyed when they saw the master.

[21]'Peace be with you,' he said to them again. 'As the father has sent me, so I'm sending you.'

[22]With that, he breathed on them.

'Receive the holy spirit,' he said. [23]'If you forgive anyone's sins, they are forgiven. If you retain anyone's sins, they are retained.'

'I couldn't possibly do that!'

He stood staring at the committee. They had just offered him, not the job he had applied for, but the one above it. The senior position in the whole division. He would be running an entire department. A huge budget. Overseeing a wide range of the company's operations. He simply wasn't up to it.

'Well,' said the chairman, 'we think you can. Of course it's going to be a big responsibility. But we can help you. We believe you're the right person for the job, and we're going to change some things around so you get the right assistance. The specialist advice. All of that. You'll have everything you need so you can do it.'

Now read verse 23. 'If you forgive anyone's sins, they are forgiven.' How do you feel about that? Are you up to the job? Of course not! But worse is to come. 'If you retain anyone's sins, they are retained!' If anyone imagines they are ready and willing to take on *that* task, they need to go back to school for a few strong lessons in humility.

But Jesus thinks the **disciples** can do it. Indeed, he's not asking them if they would like to; he's giving them a command. They are to go and do it.

But of course that's not the whole story. They could come back at him and say, 'But we thought only God could forgive sins!' And they'd be right. God is going to forgive sins – *through them*. The command comes after the crucial promise and gift: 'Receive the **holy spirit**.'

The holy spirit! Jesus has said so much already about this spirit, his own spirit, the spirit which is the father's special gift to his people. Now the time has come.

The point of receiving the holy spirit, it's clear, is not to give the disciples new 'spiritual experiences', though to be sure they will have plenty. Nor is it to set them apart from ordinary people, a sort of holier-than-thou club – though to be sure they are called to live the rich, full life of devotion and dedication that is modelled on Jesus' own. The point is so that they can do, in and for the whole world, what Jesus had been doing in Israel. 'As the father has sent me, so I'm sending you' (verse 21).

That's the clue to it all. How does the unique achievement of Jesus, in one time and place, affect all other times and places? How does the **message** he preached, which made so much sense in first-century Palestine, spread to other cultures and peoples who aren't thinking about God's **kingdom**, who aren't waiting for a **Messiah**, who don't look at the world like that at all?

'Salvation is from the Jews' (4.22). *From* Israel, *for* the world. The long story of God and Israel has reached its climax in Jesus. Now the salvation he has brought to Israel is to come *from* the Jewish world, out to the wider world of the **Gentiles**. And the disciples are to start the process of taking it there.

There is all the difference in the world between something being achieved and something being implemented. The composer achieves the writing of the music; the performers implement it. The clockmaker designs and builds the wonderful clock. The owner now has to set it to the right time and keep it wound up. Jesus has accomplished the defeat of death, and has begun the work of new creation (notice how John again stresses that it was the first day of the week). His followers don't have to do that all over again. (This, by the way, is why the early church didn't say exactly the same things that he said. That confuses people who think that Jesus was just a great moral or spiritual teacher. They then wonder why his followers kept talking *about* him instead of simply repeating what he had said. The answer is that they were implementing his achievement, not trying to duplicate it. That would have been the real disloyalty.)

Jesus' mission to Israel, reaching its climax in his death and **resurrection**, is thus to be implemented by the disciples' mission to the world. That's why they need the holy spirit: Jesus' breath, God's breath, to enable them to do the job they could otherwise never dream of doing.

The theme of new creation goes deeper still into this passage. When God came looking for Adam in the garden (Genesis 3.8), he and his wife heard the sound of him at the time of the evening breeze. Now, on the evening of the new creation's first day, a different wind sweeps through the room. The words for 'wind', 'breath' and 'spirit' are the same (this is true in both Hebrew and Greek). This wind is the healing breath of God's spirit, come to undo the long effects of primal rebellion.

This takes us back to the moment of creation itself. In Genesis 2.7 God breathed into human nostrils his own breath, the breath of **life**, and humankind became alive, alive with God's life. Now, in the new creation, the restoring life of God is breathed out through Jesus, making new people of the disciples, and, through them, offering this new life to the world.

The result is that peace, twice repeated here, which Jesus had promised in 14.27 and 16.33. With that peace, they are enabled to perform the extraordinary task we began with (verse 23). They are to pronounce, in God's name and by his spirit, the message of forgiveness to all who believe in Jesus. They are also to 'retain sins': to warn the world that sin is a serious, deadly disease, and that to remain in it will bring death. They are to rebuke and warn – not because they don't like people, or because they are seeking power or prestige for themselves, but because this is God's message to a muddled, confused and still rebellious world.

Paul, twenty years later, asked, 'Who is sufficient for such things?' (2 Corinthians 2.16). He, like John, gave the right answer: none of us, but God enables us to do it by his spirit.

JOHN 20.24–31

Jesus and Thomas

[24]One of the Twelve, Thomas (also known as Didymus), wasn't with them when Jesus came. [25]So the other disciples spoke to him.

'We've seen the master!' they said.

'Unless I see the mark of the nails in his hands,' replied Thomas, 'and put my finger into the nail-marks, and put my hand into his side – I'm not going to believe!'

[26]A week later the disciples were again in the house, and Thomas was with them. The doors were shut. Jesus came and stood in the middle of them.

'Peace be with you!' he said.

[27]Then he addressed Thomas.

'Bring your finger here', he said, 'and inspect my hands. Bring your hand here and put it into my side. Don't be faithless! Just believe!'

[28]'My master,' replied Thomas, 'and my God!'

[29]'Is it because you've seen me that you believe?' replied Jesus. 'God's blessing on people who don't see, and yet believe!'

[30]Jesus did many other signs in the presence of his disciples, which aren't written in this book. [31]But these ones are written so that you may believe that the Messiah, the son of God, is none other than Jesus; and that, with this faith, you may have life in his name.

Out of my window I can see a clock. A large and famous clock, on a great public building. It's lit up at night, and you can see it from many parts of the city. As I write this, it has just struck the hour.

Consider the journey that the clock makes from midnight to midday. The hands start together at 12. They take their time making their separate way around the clock face. Finally they come back together again. It's the same time as it was when we started, yet it's half a day later. It's a different time because of all that has happened in between, and yet it's the same.

That feeling of same-but-different, of coming round the circle and ending up where we started, is what John intends us to have as his book comes to its original ending. (As we shall see in the next section, it looks likely that chapter 21 was added some time after the original book had been completed.) With this story of Thomas, and also with chapter 20 as a whole, what John set out to tell us in his **gospel**, from those unforgettable opening lines onwards, has been completed. The story has taken its time working this way and that. We have met many interesting characters and watched them interact with Jesus. Some have misunderstood him. Some have been downright hostile. Some (often to their own surprise) have come to believe in him. We now have another such character to add to John's vivid collection of portraits. He, Thomas, brings the book round to where we started, with his breathtaking statement of new-found **faith**.

'My master,' he says, 'and my God!' He is the first person in this book to look at Jesus of Nazareth and address the word 'God' directly to him. Yet this is what John has been working round to from the beginning. 'In the beginning was the **Word** . . . and the Word was God.' 'Nobody has ever seen God. The only-begotten God, who is intimately close to the father – he has brought him to light.' What does that mean? What does it look like when it's actually happening? Well, says John, it looks like this . . . and off we go, through Galilee and Jerusalem, back and forth, moments of glory and doom woven together until they meet on the cross. Now, a week after Easter, it looks like this: a muddled, dogged **disciple**, determined not to be taken in, standing on his rights not to believe anything until he's got solid evidence, confronted by a smiling Jesus who has just walked, as he did the previous week, through a locked door. This is what it looks like.

And of course it baffled Thomas just as it baffles us. What sort of a person – what sort of an *object* – are we dealing with here? The whole point of the story is that it's the same Jesus. The marks of the nails in his hands. The wound in his side, big enough to get your hand into. This isn't a ghost. Nor is it someone else pretending to be Jesus. This is him. This is the body that the grave-cloths couldn't contain any longer.

But he has not only escaped death, the grave, the cloths and the spices. He comes and goes as though he belongs *both* in our world *and* in a different world, one which intersects with ours at various points but doesn't use the same geography. If this is fiction, it is the oddest fiction ever written. And John certainly doesn't intend it as fiction.

Thomas, bless him, acts as we would expect. (It is in this gospel that the rather flat characters in the other accounts come up in more three-dimensional reality.) The dour, dogged disciple who suggested they might as well go with Jesus, if only to die with him (11.16), who complained that Jesus hadn't made things anything like clear enough (14.5), just happened to be the one who was somewhere else on the first Easter day. He sees the others excited, elated, unable to contain their joy. He's not going to be taken in.

Fair enough. At the end, Jesus issues a gentle rebuke to Thomas for needing to see before he would believe; but we notice that the beloved disciple describes his own arrival at faith in the same way. 'He saw, and believed' (verse 8). This isn't, then, so much a rebuke to Thomas; it's more an encouragement to those who come later, to people of subsequent generations. We are all 'blessed' when, without having seen the risen Lord for ourselves, we nevertheless believe in him.

If the Word who was God has now made the invisible God visible, so, as in the Prologue, this chapter has described how he has brought **life** and light to the world. The **resurrection** is not an alien power breaking into God's world; it is what happens when the creator himself comes to heal and restore his world, and bring it to its appointed goal. The resurrection is not only *new* creation; it is new *creation*.

To grasp this is vital for the health of the Christian faith. Any sense that Jesus starts a movement which is somehow opposed to, or can leave behind, the world God made in the first place is excluded by this gospel from start to finish. The wheel has come full circle. The clock has returned to where it began. We have, as T. S. Eliot said, arrived at the place where we started, to discover that now we know it for the first time.

And, as the rest of chapter 1 after the Prologue (i.e. verses 19–51) have as their central theme the surprising discovery that the **Messiah**, the **son of God**, is none other than Jesus of Nazareth, so John concludes this chapter by insisting that, out of the great mass of material he could have selected, he has chosen these 'signs' so that we, his readers, may come to that faith for ourselves. The first half of verse 31 is often translated the other way round ('that you may know that Jesus is the Messiah, the son of God'); but the grammar of the original sentence points firmly in the same direction as chapter 1, to which all this looks back.

John isn't saying that the early disciples were confronted with Jesus and tried to find a category for him. That's no doubt true as well, but it's not the point he's making. He is saying that they, first-century Jews as they were, were looking for a Messiah, and discovered that it was Jesus.

Jesus, of course, remodelled the meaning of messiahship

around himself. That's what the book is all about. But the underlying point is not just to get categories and definitions straightened out. The point is to believe in Jesus, and so, through this faith, to have life in his name. 'In him was life'; yes, and it can be in you too.

JOHN 21.1–8

Jesus on the Beach

[1]After this, Jesus showed himself again to the disciples by the sea of Tiberias. This was how he showed himself.

[2]Simon Peter, Thomas (known as Didymus), Nathanael from Cana in Galilee, the sons of Zebedee, and two other disciples, were all together.

[3]Simon Peter spoke up.

'I'm going fishing,' he said.

'We'll go with you,' they replied.

So they went off and got into the boat; but that night they caught nothing.

[4]As dawn was breaking, Jesus stood beside the seashore, but the disciples didn't know that it was Jesus.

[5]'Children,' said Jesus to them, 'haven't you caught anything worth eating?'

'No!' they replied.

[6]'Cast the net on the right side of the boat,' he said, 'and you'll find something.'

So they cast the net; and now they couldn't draw it in because of the weight of the fish.

[7]So the disciple that Jesus loved spoke to Peter.

'It's the master!' he said.

When Simon Peter heard that it was the master, he wrapped his cloak around him (he had been naked for work), and threw himself into the sea. [8]The other disciples brought the boat in to land, dragging the net full of fish. They weren't far from shore, about a hundred yards away.

The level of the lake has dropped now, but you can still sense what a lovely place it is. So much water is now taken out of the Sea of Galilee, and the River Jordan which feeds it and then flows from it, that even in the fifteen years since I first stood on this spot the water has receded, leaving a hundred yards or so of reeds and pebbles between the old shoreline and the new. But you can still get a sense, in the little place called Tabgha, just west of Capernaum, of what it must have been like that morning.

It was, and still is when the tourists aren't there, a quiet place, on the north shore of the sea. It's quite a distance from the major town of Tiberias. It is still enough to hear the water lapping at your feet. The colour of the sky, reflected in the lake, gives you double the effect of the spectacular sunrise, the great fiery ball coming up over the Golan Heights. The day dawns full of new beauty and possibility. That is part of what John is telling us in this story (notice how, once more, he draws our attention to dawn, in verse 4, as he points to the risen Jesus).

Why had they gone fishing? It's a puzzle, and I suspect it was a puzzle for them too. Like half the things Peter proposed in the **gospel**, it was probably a case of the right motivation and the wrong judgment. He wanted to get on with life. To do the next thing. This was the world they knew. It would feel strange, going back to it, but they had families who needed looking after, who must have been bemused to have them back again after all their adventures, and might well have been suggesting that they should settle down and do something sensible for a change. Like earning some money. Like catching some fish.

But it didn't work. They knew the sea. They were old hands, most of them. They knew where the fish congregated, where you could normally find shoals. And, as in Luke 5.4–7, they worked all night and took nothing. They knew, as fishermen do know, that if you don't make a catch at night you're far less likely to by day.

But, just as dawn was breaking, and the sky and the sea were filling with colour, and they were stretching and shivering and feeling tired and ready for food and rest – at that moment he came again. Like Mary in the garden, they didn't know it was him. But they soon did. A word of greeting, a word of command – sometimes people on shore can see better than people in a boat where the shoal is, but there is no reason to rationalize this story away – and the nets were filled. Like the two **disciples** in the house at Emmaus (Luke 24.31), they knew in a flash who it was.

It might have been easier for Peter if, as happened on that occasion, Jesus had simply vanished. But he didn't. He stayed on the shore and waited for them to come in. Peter, who longed to see Jesus again and clearly still had unfinished business with him, grabbed a cloak and leapt into the sea, once again doing the impulsive thing, this time leaving the others to do the hard work.

If it's a puzzle why they went fishing, it could be a puzzle working out why John has told this story. It seems to have been added after he'd finished the first, and main, draft of the book. We shall come back to this question in the final section, 21.20–23. John tells it partly, it seems, to set the scene for the almost unbearably tense dialogue between Jesus and Peter in verses 15–19, and the haunting question about the Beloved disciple himself in verses 21–23. But the detail of the present section suggests that it has a purpose of its own, too.

Jesus, after all, has given his followers a strange and striking commission in chapter 20. They are to work for him. They are to be filled with God's breath, and be sent into the world as Jesus had been. But if they try to do it their own way, they will fail. They will toil all night and take nothing. The only way is for them to admit defeat, to listen afresh to Jesus' voice, and to do what he says. Then there is no knowing what they will achieve.

Stand in your mind's eye with the disciples in the boat. What projects have you been labouring over, and getting nowhere? Watch for the dawn. Watch for the figure on the shore. Listen for his voice. And then do whatever he tells you.

JOHN 21.9–14

Breakfast by the Shore

[9]When they came to land, they saw a charcoal fire laid there, with fish and bread on it.

[10]Jesus spoke to them.

'Bring some of the fish you've just caught,' he said.

[11]So Simon Peter went and pulled the net onto the shore. It was full of large fish, a hundred and fifty-three in all. The net wasn't torn, even though there were so many.

[12]'Come and have breakfast,' said Jesus to them.

None of the disciples dared ask him, 'Who are you?' They knew it was the master.

[13]Jesus came and took the bread and gave it to them, and so also with the fish. [14]This was now the third time that Jesus had appeared to the disciples after he had been raised from the dead.

I don't know much about mental health, and the therapy that can produce it. But I do know a little about the healing of memories, and the finding of a forgiveness that can go back to a buried hurt, fear, failure or sin and deal with it. I have had the privilege of working pastorally with people, and watching as a deep unhealed wound was gently exposed, dealt with in love and prayer, and enabled at last to find healing.

That's one of the things that is going on in this chapter. And it begins with the charcoal fire.

Remember the two passages that bring us to this point. In

chapter 13, Peter insists, loudly and emphatically, that he at least will remain loyal to Jesus. He's not going to let him down. He wants to follow him wherever he goes: to prison, to death, wherever. In fact, he is prepared to lay down his own life on Jesus' behalf (13.36–37). Then, in chapter 18, we watch helplessly as Peter tries and fails. He follows, but when he gets there it all goes horribly wrong. Then, instead of getting out quickly before worse occurs, he stays and gets it wrong again. And again. Three times he denies that he's one of Jesus' followers (*one of*? He's supposed to be their Number One). And the cock crows.

And it all happens beside a charcoal fire. Think back to the smell of that fire, wafting through the chilly April air. Think of Peter going out in shame, angry with himself, knowing that Jesus knew. Knowing that the 'beloved **disciple**' knew. Knowing that God knew. And hearing the next day what had happened to Jesus. Not even the **resurrection** itself could wave a magic wand and get rid of that memory. Nothing could, except revisiting it and bathing it in God's own healing.

The charcoal fire is the start of it, and it seems from the conversation in the next section that Jesus planned it that way. But for the moment there are – well, I was going to say there are other fish to fry. That's the point. They have caught a massive netfull: 153 fish in all, more by some way than the nets would normally hold. Enough for breakfast for the whole village.

But then there comes an interesting little exchange. Jesus is already cooking fish and bread on his charcoal fire. He doesn't need their catch. He is well capable of looking after himself (though what 'needs' his risen body now has are past our comprehension). John, describing this scene, isn't wasting words. He isn't filling in time. John never pads out stories. He is telling us something, something about working under Jesus' direction, something about the relation of our work to his.

How dreadfully easy it is for Christian workers to get the impression that we've got to do it all. God, we imagine, is waiting passively for us to get on with things. If we don't organize it, it won't happen. If we don't tell people the **good news**, they won't hear it. If we don't change the world, it won't be changed. 'He has no hands but our hands', we are sometimes told.

What a load of rubbish. Whose hands made the sun rise this morning? Whose breath guided us to think, and pray, and love, and hope? Who is the Lord of the world, anyway? We may be given the **holy spirit** to enable us to work for Jesus; but the holy breath is not independent of the master who breathes it out, of the sovereign God, the creator. Neither the institutional church nor its individual members can upstage him. Jesus welcomes Peter's catch. He asks him to bring some of it. But he doesn't, in that sense, *need* it.

Of course we are to work hard. Of course we are to be organized. Of course there is no excuse for laziness, sloppiness, half-heartedness in the **kingdom of God**. If it's God's work we're doing, we must do it with all our might. But let's have no nonsense about it all being up to us, about poor old Jesus being unable to lift a finger unless we lift it for him. In fact, we are much more likely to work effectively once we get rid of that paranoia-inducing notion. Jesus remains sovereign. Thank God for that.

Once again, as when Jesus emerged through the locked doors of the upper room, there is a moment where our spines tingle. 'None of them dared ask, Who are you? They knew it was the master' (verse 12). That is a very, very strange way to put it. It belongs with the other exceedingly strange things that are said in the resurrection accounts. They knew it was him . . . yet they wanted to ask, and were afraid to.

Why did they want to ask? They had been with him night and day for two or three years, and they wanted to ask who he was? I might as well wake up my own wife one morning and ask her who she is. If they didn't know him by now they never would.

And yet. The sentence only makes sense if Jesus is, as well as the same, somehow different. No source mentions what he was wearing. No source describes his face. Somehow he had passed through death, and into a strange new world where nobody had ever been before, and nobody has yet been since – though we are firmly and securely promised that we shall join him there eventually. His body was no longer subject to decay or death. What might that have been like?

We have no means of knowing. We are in the same position that someone in the sixteenth century would have been in if they'd been shown a computer logging on to the Internet. They hadn't got electricity in those days, let alone microchips! The difference between our present body and Jesus' risen body is like that only more so. This is a whole new world. It isn't magic. It isn't ghostly. It's real, but it's different. God help us if we ever imagine that our normal everyday world is the sum total of all that there is. What a dull, flat, boring idea.

We must always be ready to be surprised by God. They were, that spring morning, the third time they saw him after his resurrection (did John choose, in adding this chapter, to tell a third story in order to complete a kind of perfection, as with his seven signs?). They were surprised by the huge catch. (Does John see a symbolic value in the 153 fish? Possibly. It may, by a complex piece of mathematics, stand for the completeness of the 'catch' that the **apostles** will make when they take the **gospel** into the world. That doesn't mean that there weren't 153 fish, only that by now virtually everything John says may bear different levels of meaning.) They were surprised by Jesus himself. And they were surprised, we may suppose, at themselves. Who were they? What were they doing? What was to happen next? When God ceases to surprise us, that may be the moment we have ceased to do business with him.

161

JOHN 21.15–19

Jesus and Peter

¹⁵So when they had eaten breakfast, Jesus spoke to Simon Peter.

'Simon, son of John,' he said, 'do you love me more than these?'

'Yes, master,' he said. 'You know I love you.'

'Well, then,' he said, 'feed my lambs.'

¹⁶'Simon, son of John,' said Jesus again, for a second time, 'do you love me?'

'Yes, master,' he said. 'You know I love you.'

'Well, then,' he said, 'look after my sheep.'

¹⁷'Simon, son of John,' said Jesus a third time, 'do you love me?'

Peter was upset that he asked a third time, 'Do you love me?'

'Master,' he said, 'you know everything! You know I love you!'

'Well, then,' said Jesus, 'feed my sheep.'

¹⁸'I'm telling you the solemn truth,' he went on. 'When you were young, you put on your own clothes and went about wherever you wanted. But when you are old, you'll stretch out your hands, and someone else will dress you up and take you where you don't want to go.'

¹⁹He said this to indicate what sort of death Peter would die to bring God glory. And when he had said this, he added, 'Follow me!'

He had offered to help clear up after the dinner party. Indeed, he was eager to do so. We gave him a towel and he worked away with us, wiping pans and jugs. But he was still excited after the events of the day, and his mind wasn't really on the job. Once or twice we suggested he might like to sit down, to read or relax. But he wanted to go on.

Then it happened. He picked up the new crystal water jug that we'd been given a few weeks before. He began to wipe it, but as he did so he turned round to say something to the others. He didn't notice one of them turning towards him at the same moment . . . until it was too late.

He was crestfallen. We were devastated but tried not to show it. He swept up the broken glass off the floor. He promised to buy us another jug. He left, a little later, in a flood of apologies.

We struggled to think through what forgiveness would mean in a case like that. We were angry, of course, but we knew it had happened because he was just too eager for his own good. We thought about it a lot. Then, a couple of weeks later, we invited him to a meal again. And this time, after the meal, we invited him to help us clear up. Again we gave him a towel. He looked at us with a stare of disbelief. We smiled. He helped. It was fine.

This scene between Jesus and Peter is one of the most spectacular interchanges in the whole Bible, perhaps in all literature. The most remarkable thing about it is that, by way of forgiveness, Jesus gives Peter a job to do. When Peter professes his love, Jesus doesn't say, 'Well, that's all right, then.' He says, 'Well, then: feed my lambs. Look after my sheep. Feed my sheep.'

The three questions correspond to Peter's three denials. Three for completeness, yes, but three also for reminder. The smell of the charcoal fire lingers. Peter's night of agony – and Jesus' own night of agony – returns. But because of the latter, the former can be dealt with. Jesus is the Passover lamb who takes away the sin of the world, Peter's sin included, your sin, my sin.

But the way in which this taking away of sin is put into practice varies from individual to individual, and from case to case. It isn't just a matter of a divine decree being issued, wiping the slate clean. From a legal point of view (to the extent that legal points of view are helpful here; John sometimes speaks like that, and so does Paul, but law is not the only thing at stake in this context) that may be fine. There is nothing officially 'on the record' against us. But there may still be plenty in our memories and imaginations: old failings, old sores, old wounds. Like a computer with faulty and virus-ridden software on the hard disk, we need to have it dealt with before we can operate to maximum efficiency once more.

So Jesus goes to where the pain is, as he so often does (is this why so many resist his gentle advance, like someone putting off seeing the dentist until they can bear the toothache no longer?). He takes Simon Peter away from the others; as we see in verse 20, the beloved **disciple** is following them at a distance. They are probably walking slowly along the shore. And he asks the question that goes to the heart of it all: 'Do you love me?'

Actually, the words he uses vary slightly. When Peter replies, the word he uses for 'love' is different to the one Jesus uses in the first two questions. Then, in the third question, Jesus uses the word Peter himself had been using. But this is probably not important. John does say, after all, that the same question was being asked three times over (verse 17). What matters is that the question is asked and answered; and, even more, that the answer earns, each time, not a pat on the back, not a 'There, that's all right then', but a command. A fresh challenge. A new commission. Time to learn how to be a shepherd. Time to feed lambs and sheep, to look after them.

Not only is this a fresh commission. Not only is Jesus trusting Peter to get back to fruitful work, and to turn his undoubted though hitherto wobbly love for Jesus to good account. It is more: Jesus is sharing his own work, his own ministry, with Peter.

It is, after all, Jesus who is the 'good shepherd' (chapter 10). It is Jesus who has the task of leading and feeding his sheep and lambs, guiding them to and from pasture, keeping them safe from predators. He knows them and they know him. He has now given his life for them. But the commission of 20.21 was quite specific. '*As* the father sent me, *so* I'm sending you.' There's no getting away from it. And this is what it means. Peter is to share Jesus' task of shepherding.

Here is the secret of all Christian ministry, yours and mine, lay and ordained, full-time or part-time. It's the secret of everything from being a quiet, back-row member of a prayer group to being a platform speaker at huge rallies and conferences. If you are going to do any single solitary thing as a follower and servant of Jesus, this is what it's built on. Somewhere, deep down inside, there is a love for Jesus, and though (goodness knows) you've let him down enough times, he wants to find that love, to give you a chance to express it, to heal the hurts and failures of the past, and give you new work to do.

These are not things for you to do to 'earn' the forgiveness. Nothing can ever do that. It is grace from start to finish. They are things to do out of the joy and relief that you already *are* forgiven. Things we are given to do precisely as the sign that we are forgiven. Things that will be costly, because Jesus' own work was utterly costly. Things that will mean following Jesus into suffering, perhaps into death. In the last week, as I have been writing this, more Christians have been killed around the world, simply for worshipping Jesus. 'Someone else will dress you and take you where you would rather not go.' Peter will complete his task as a shepherd by laying down his own life, in turn, for the sheep.

But even this is not something different from the call that drew the disciples in the first place. 'Follow me!' Now that Jesus has taken the steep road to the cross, and has proved that death itself is defeated by the life and joy of the new creation, he can ask for everything from those he has rescued, and know he will get it.

Peter went from strength to strength. He was still muddled from time to time, as Acts indicates. But he became a shepherd. He loved Jesus and looked after his sheep. No one could ask for more. Jesus never asks for less.

JOHN 21.20–25

The Beloved Disciple

20Peter turned and saw, following them, the disciple that Jesus loved. This was the disciple who had leaned close beside Jesus at the supper, and had asked, 'Master, who is it who's going to betray you?'

21'Master,' said Peter to Jesus, seeing him there, 'what about him?'

22'If it's my intention', replied Jesus, 'that he should remain here until I come, what's that got to do with you? You must follow me!'

23So the rumour went around the Christian family that this disciple wouldn't die. But Jesus didn't say he wouldn't die. What he said, rather, was this: 'If it's my intention that he should remain here until I come, what's that got to do with you?'

24(This is the disciple who is giving evidence about these things, and who wrote them down. We know that his evidence is true.)

25There are many other things which Jesus did. If they were written down one by one, I don't think the world itself would be able to contain the books that would be written.

They came back almost in despair from the dress rehearsal. The costumes were ridiculous. The set was bizarre. The director seemed to have no real idea of how the action would work on stage. Even with an opera, where the music is what really matters, it's important that the actors are doing *something*, not just standing around.

But worst of all was the casting. The singer they had gone to support had an important part. But it just wasn't her. The character in the story was so different from her. There was nothing natural about it. She would have been better in a minor part, playing something that suited her temperament.

The theme of the last section in John's **gospel** is the quite different parts that two of the main actors are now going to play. Peter and the beloved **disciple** have been on stage for much of the action so far. In particular, they have been important at the supper in chapter 13, at the arrest and trial in chapter 18, and in the **resurrection** accounts in chapters 20 and 21. But now their paths are going to diverge; and it is no part of the vocation of either of them to look over their shoulder and wonder why the other one is different.

Peter's question, though, is quite natural. He and John (if it is John) have had so much to do, side by side. Now Jesus has told him, Peter, that he is going to have to follow him, not only in being a shepherd to the flock, but in glorifying God through dying as a martyr (verses 18–19). It is the most natural thing in the world that he should ask Jesus whether John will share this fate too.

But the most important thing, for the future, is for both of them to learn that God makes no mistakes in casting. Oh, it feels like that from time to time, no doubt. There are many times when faithful Christians look with puzzlement, and (alas) envy, at one another, and wish that they could swap places. But part of Christian obedience, part of accepting our commission as the language of our forgiveness (verses 15–17), is knowing that we are called to follow Jesus wherever he leads *us*, not wherever he leads the person next to us.

The fate of John is, in fact, the most likely reason why chapter 21 was added to the book. In order to get to the point (verse 23), the writer had to tell the whole story of the fishing trip, the seaside breakfast and the conversation between Jesus and Peter. Without that, the comment in verse 22 would have made no sense.

So what was going on? One possibility is that the author was getting near death, and knew that there was no reason, in anything Jesus had said, why he should not die as all the other original **apostles** had died. But a rumour had gone around in the early church, based on a misunderstanding of what Jesus had said to Peter, that John would be the one original apostle who would remain alive until the Lord returned. (The return of Jesus isn't mentioned elsewhere in the book, but this shows that it was assumed throughout.)

We may suppose, then, that the elderly apostle, or someone else at his dictation and suggestion, wrote chapter 21 and added it to the book that had already been finished. Indeed, verse 24 looks like a note from somebody else, either a **scribe** or a close friend, to certify that the beloved disciple really was the author, and could be trusted. The new version of the book could then be circulated, after the death of the beloved disciple, to make it clear that this had not upset Jesus' intentions.

Jesus had never meant to say anything definite about what *would* happen to John. He had only meant to say something definite about the fact that it was none of Peter's business. I might say to a child, 'Please come and help me in the garden.' The child, dragging her feet, might look at her brother and say, 'What's *he* going to do?' And I might answer, 'Supposing I want him to fly to the moon for me, what's that got to do with you?' That doesn't mean that I really *do* want him to fly to the moon. Jesus didn't say that John would stay alive until his return. He only said it was none of Peter's business.

John, or perhaps the trusted friend who put all this together after his death, knows that the book already has a proper conclusion in 20.30–31. But he finds a way of writing another one that is almost as good. It starts off in much the same way: there are many other things that Jesus did. (We should remember that, like most people telling a story, our author has selected as well as arranged. Very few people write down everything that they *might* have written, every single thing that they know about a person or a topic.) But this time, instead of telling us why he has written the things he has, he tells us what would have happened if he'd tried to write down all the other ones too. 'The world itself wouldn't be able to contain the books that would be written.'

Well, we know of larger libraries, and of very much larger electronic storing systems, than anything a first-century author could have imagined. But that is hardly the point. Even if it might be technically true that every single deed Jesus ever did could be written down, and that the books, though numerous, would ultimately be finite in number, nevertheless the point remains: *the world* wouldn't be able to contain them. They would be too explosive. It would be like trying to play a wonderful symphony on a broken piano. It would be like trying to serve a gourmet meal in a snack bar. It would be like God's breath inside an ordinary human being. It would be like light shining in darkness, and the darkness being unable to master it. The world couldn't take it.

But the ultimate point is this. Once the **Word** has become flesh, all the books in the world can't do justice to it. Nothing less than flesh can now do justice to the meaning of the Word: your flesh, my flesh. Books can reach a small way out into the world. Our lives, in the power of the **spirit**, can reach a lot further. Jesus' disciples are sent into 'the world', not just in the first century, but in every generation. 'The world' remains the object of God's saving love, the reason why Jesus died (3.16). He was sent into it by the father, and now he sends us. And whatever part we are called to play, we go to it with his words (16.33) ringing in our ears:

'You'll have trouble in the world. But cheer up! I have defeated the world!'

GLOSSARY

accuser, *see* **the satan**

age to come, *see* **present age**

apostle, disciple, the Twelve

'Apostle' means 'one who is sent'. It could be used of an ambassador or official delegate. In the New Testament it is sometimes used specifically of Jesus' inner circle of twelve; but Paul sees not only himself but several others outside the Twelve as 'apostles', the criterion being whether the person had personally seen the risen Jesus. Jesus' own choice of twelve close associates symbolized his plan to renew God's people, Israel; after the death of Judas Iscariot (Matthew 27.5; Acts 1.18) Matthias was chosen by lot to take his place, preserving the symbolic meaning. During Jesus' lifetime they, and many other followers, were seen as his 'disciples', which means 'pupils' or 'apprentices'.

baptism

Literally, 'plunging' people into water. From within a wider Jewish tradition of ritual washings and bathings, **John the Baptist** undertook a vocation of baptizing people in the Jordan, not as one ritual among others but as a unique moment of **repentance**, preparing them for the coming of the **kingdom of God**. Jesus himself was baptized by John, identifying himself with this renewal movement and developing it in his own way. His followers in turn baptized others. After his **resurrection**, and the sending of the **holy spirit**, baptism became the normal sign and means of entry into the community of Jesus' people. As early as Paul it was aligned both with the **Exodus** from Egypt (1 Corinthians 10.2) and with Jesus' death and resurrection (Romans 6.2–11).

Christ, *see* Messiah

circumcision, circumcised

The cutting off of the foreskin. Male circumcision was a major mark of identity for Jews, following its initial commandment to Abraham (Genesis 17), reinforced by Joshua (Joshua 5.2–9). Other peoples, e.g. the Egyptians, also circumcised male children. A line of thought from Deuteronomy (e.g. 30.6), through Jeremiah (e.g. 31.33), to the **Dead Sea Scrolls** and the New Testament (e.g. Romans 2.29) speaks of 'circumcision of the heart' as God's real desire, by which one may become inwardly what the male Jew is outwardly, that is, marked out as part of God's people. At periods of Jewish assimilation into the surrounding culture, some Jews tried to remove the marks of circumcision (e.g. 1 Maccabees 1.11–15).

covenant

At the heart of Jewish belief is the conviction that the one God, YHWH, who had made the whole world, had called Abraham and his family to belong to him in a special way. The promises God made to Abraham and his family, and the requirements that were laid on them as a result, came to be seen in terms either of the agreement that a king would make with a subject people, or sometimes of the marriage bond between husband and wife. One regular way of describing this relationship was 'covenant', which can thus include both promise and **law**. The covenant was renewed at Mount Sinai with the giving of the **Torah**; in Deuteronomy before the entry to the promised land; and, in a more focused way, with David (e.g. Psalm 89). Jeremiah 31 promised that after the punishment of **exile** God would make a 'new covenant' with his people, forgiving them and binding them to him more intimately. Jesus believed that this was coming true through his **kingdom**-proclamation and his death and **resurrection**. The early Christians developed these ideas in various ways, believing that in Jesus the promises had at last been fulfilled.

Dead Sea Scrolls

A collection of texts, some in remarkably good repair, some extremely fragmentary, found in the late 1940s around Qumran (near the northeast corner of the Dead Sea), and virtually all now edited, translated and in the public domain. They formed all or part of the library of a strict monastic group, most likely Essenes, founded in the mid-second century BC and lasting until the Jewish–Roman war of 66–70. The scrolls include the earliest existing manuscripts of the Hebrew and Aramaic scriptures, and several other important documents of community regulations, scriptural exegesis, hymns, wisdom writings, and other literature. They shed a flood of light on one small segment within the Judaism of Jesus' day, helping us to understand how some Jews at least were thinking, praying and reading scripture. Despite attempts to prove the contrary, they make no reference to **John the Baptist**, Jesus, Paul, James or early Christianity in general.

demons, *see* **the satan**

devil, *see* **the satan**

disciple, *see* **apostle**

Essenes, *see* **Dead Sea Scrolls**

eternal life, *see* **present age**

eucharist

The meal in which the earliest Christians, and Christians ever since, obeyed Jesus' command to 'do this in remembrance of him' at the Last Supper (Luke 22.19; 1 Corinthians 11.23–26). The word 'eucharist' itself comes from the Greek for 'thanksgiving'; it means, basically, 'the thank-you meal', and looks back to the many times when Jesus took bread, gave thanks for it, broke it, and gave it to people (e.g. Luke 24.30; John 6.11). Other early phrases for the same meal are 'the Lord's supper' (1 Corinthians 11.20) and 'the breaking of bread' (Acts 2.42). Later it came to be called 'the Mass' (from the Latin word at the end of the service, meaning 'sent out') and 'Holy Communion' (Paul speaks of 'sharing' or 'communion' in the body and blood of Christ). Later theological controversies about the precise meaning of the various actions and elements of the meal should not obscure its centrality in earliest Christian living and its continuing vital importance today.

exile

Deuteronomy (29—30) warned that if Israel disobeyed YHWH, he would send his people into exile, but that if they then repented he would bring them back. When the Babylonians sacked Jerusalem and took the people into exile, prophets such as Jeremiah interpreted this as the fulfilment of this prophecy, and made further promises about how long exile would last (70 years, according to Jeremiah 25.12; 29.10). Sure enough, exiles began to return in the late sixth century (Ezra 1.1). However, the post-exilic period was largely a disappointment, since the people were still enslaved to foreigners (Nehemiah 9.36); and at the height of persecution by the Syrians, Daniel 9.2, 24 spoke of the 'real' exile lasting not for 70 years but for 70 *weeks* of years, i.e., 490 years. Longing for the real 'return from exile', when the prophecies of Isaiah, Jeremiah, etc. would be fulfilled, and redemption from pagan oppression accomplished, continued to characterize many Jewish movements, and was a major theme in Jesus' proclamation and his summons to **repentance**.

Exodus

The Exodus from Egypt took place, according to the book of that name, under the leadership of Moses, after long years in which the Israelites had been enslaved there. (According to Genesis 15.13f., this was itself part of God's covenanted promise to Abraham.) It demonstrated, to them and to Pharaoh, King of Egypt, that Israel was God's special child (Exodus 4.22). They then wandered through the Sinai wilderness for 40 years, led by God in a pillar of cloud and fire; early on in this time they were given the **Torah** on Mount Sinai itself. Finally, after the death of Moses and under the leadership of Joshua, they crossed the Jordan and entered, and eventually conquered, the promised land of Canaan. This event, commemorated annually in Passover and other Jewish festivals, gave the Israelites not only a powerful memory of what had made them a people, but also a particular shape and content to their faith in YHWH as not only creator but also redeemer; and in subsequent enslavements, particularly the **exile**, they looked for a further redemption which would be, in effect, a new Exodus. Probably no other past event so dominated the imagination of first-century Jews; among them the early Christians, following the lead of Jesus himself, continually referred back to the Exodus to give meaning and shape to their own critical events, most particularly Jesus' death and **resurrection**.

faith

Faith in the New Testament covers a wide area of human trust and trustworthiness, merging into love at one end of the scale and loyalty at the other. Within Jewish and Christian thinking faith in God also includes *belief,* accepting certain things as true about God, and what he has done in the world (e.g. bringing Israel out of Egypt; raising Jesus from the dead). For Jesus, 'faith' often seems to mean 'recognizing that God is decisively at work to bring the **kingdom** through Jesus'. For Paul, 'faith' is both the specific belief that Jesus is Lord and that God raised him from the dead (Romans 10.9) and the response of grateful human love to sovereign divine love (Galatians 2.20). This faith is, for Paul, the solitary badge of membership in God's people in **Christ**, marking them out in a way that **Torah**, and the works it prescribes, can never do.

Gentiles

The Jews divided the world into Jews and non-Jews. The Hebrew word for non-Jews, *goyim,* carries overtones both of family identity (i.e., not of Jewish ancestry) and of worship (i.e., of idols, not of the one true God YHWH). Though many Jews established good relations with Gentiles, not least in the Jewish Diaspora (the dispersion of Jews away from Palestine), officially there were taboos against contact such as intermarriage. In the New Testament the Greek word *ethne,* 'nations', carries the same meanings as *goyim.* Part of Paul's overmastering agenda was to insist that Gentiles who believed in Jesus had full rights in the Christian community alongside believing Jews, without having to become **circumcised**.

good news, gospel, message, word

The idea of 'good news', for which an older English word is 'gospel', had two principal meanings for first-century Jews. First, with roots in Isaiah, it meant the news of YHWH's long-awaited victory over evil and rescue of his people. Second, it was used in the Roman world of the accession, or birthday, or the emperor. Since for Jesus and Paul the announcement of God's inbreaking **kingdom** was both the fulfilment of prophecy and a challenge to the world's present rulers, 'gospel' became an important shorthand for both the message of Jesus himself, and the apostolic message about him. Paul saw this message as itself the vehicle of God's saving power (Romans 1.16; 1 Thessalonians 2.13).

The four canonical 'gospels' tell the story of Jesus in such a way as to bring out both these aspects (unlike some other so-called 'gospels' circulated in the second and subsequent centuries, which tended both to cut off the scriptural and Jewish roots of Jesus' achievement and to inculcate a private spirituality rather than confrontation with the world's rulers). Since in Isaiah this creative, life-giving good news was seen as God's own powerful word (40.8; 55.11), the early Christians could use 'word' or 'message' as another shorthand for the basic Christian proclamation.

gospel, *see* **good news**

heaven

Heaven is God's dimension of the created order (Genesis 1.1; Psalm 115.16; Matthew 6.9), whereas 'earth' is the world of space, time and matter that we know. 'Heaven' thus sometimes stands, reverentially, for 'God' (as in Matthew's regular '**kingdom** of heaven'). Normally hidden from human sight, heaven is occasionally revealed or unveiled so that people can see God's dimension of ordinary life (e.g. 2 Kings 6.17; Revelation 1, 4—5). Heaven in the New Testament is thus not usually seen as the place where God's people go after death; at the end the New Jerusalem descends *from* heaven *to* earth, joining the two dimensions for ever. 'Entering the kingdom of heaven' does not mean 'going to heaven after death', but belonging in the present to the people who steer their earthly course by the standards and purposes of heaven (cf. the Lord's Prayer: 'on earth as in heaven', Matthew 6. 10) and who are assured of membership in the **age to come**.

Herodians

Herod the Great ruled Judaea from 37 to 4 BC; after his death his territory was divided between his sons Archelaus, Herod Antipas (the Herod of the **gospels**), and Philip. The Herodians supported the claims of Antipas to be the true king of the Jews. Though the **Pharisees** would normally oppose such a claim, they could make common cause with the Herodians when facing a common threat (e.g. Jesus, Mark 3.6).

high priest, *see* priests

holy spirit

In Genesis 1.2, the spirit is God's presence and power *within* creation, without God being identified with creation. The same spirit entered people, notably the prophets, enabling them to speak and act for God. At his **baptism** by **John the Baptist**, Jesus was specially equipped with the spirit, resulting in his remarkable public career (Acts 10.38). After his **resurrection**, his followers were themselves filled (Acts 2) by the same spirit, now identified as Jesus' own spirit: the creator God was acting afresh, remaking the world and them too. The spirit enabled them to live out a holiness which the **Torah** could not, producing 'fruit' in their lives, giving them 'gifts' with which to serve God, the world, and the church, and assuring them of future resurrection (Romans 8; Galatians 4—5; 1 Corinthians 12—14). From very early in Christianity (e.g. Galatians 4.1–7), the spirit became part of the new revolutionary definition of God himself: 'the one who sends the son and the spirit of the son'.

John (the Baptist)

Jesus' cousin on his mother's side, born a few months before Jesus; his father was a **priest**. He acted as a prophet, baptizing in the Jordan – dramatically re-enacting the **Exodus** from Egypt – to prepare people, by **repentance**, for God's coming judgment. He may have had some contact with the **Essenes**, though his eventual public message was different from theirs. Jesus' own vocation was decisively confirmed at his **baptism** by John. As part of John's message of the **kingdom**, he outspokenly criticized Herod Antipas for marrying his brother's wife. Herod had him imprisoned, and then beheaded him at his wife's request (Mark 6.14–29). Groups of John's disciples continued a separate existence, without merging into Christianity, for some time afterwards (e.g. Acts 19.1–7).

justification

God's declaration, from his position as judge of all the world, that someone is in the right, despite universal sin. This declaration will be made on the last day on the basis of an entire life (Romans 2.1–16), but is brought forward into the present on the basis of Jesus' achievement, because sin has been dealt with through his cross (Romans 3.21—4.25); the means of this present justification is simply **faith**. This means, particularly, that Jews and **Gentiles** alike are full members of the family promised by God to Abraham (Galatians 3; Romans 4).

kingdom of God, kingdom of heaven

Best understood as the king*ship*, or sovereign and saving rule, of Israel's God **YHWH**, as celebrated in several psalms (e.g. 99.1) and prophecies (e.g. Daniel 6.26f.). Because YHWH was the creator God, when he finally became king in the way he intended this would involve setting the world to rights, and particularly rescuing Israel from its enemies. 'Kingdom of God' and various equivalents (e.g. 'No king but God!') became a revolutionary slogan around the time of Jesus. Jesus' own announcement of God's kingdom redefined these expectations around his own very different plan and vocation. His invitation to people to 'enter' the kingdom was a way of summoning them to allegiance to himself and his programme, seen as the start of God's long-awaited saving reign. For Jesus, the kingdom was coming not in a single move, but in stages, of which his own public career was one, his death and **resurrection** another, and a still future consummation another. Note that 'kingdom of **heaven**' is Matthew's preferred form for the same phrase, following a regular Jewish practice of saying 'heaven' rather than 'God'. It does not refer to a place ('heaven'), but to the fact of God's becoming king in and through Jesus and his achievement. Paul speaks of Jesus, as **Messiah**, already in possession of his kingdom, waiting to hand it over finally to the father (1 Corinthians 15.23–28; cf. Ephesians 5.5).

law, *see* Torah

legal experts, lawyers, *see* Pharisees

leper, leprosy

In a world without modern medicine, tight medical controls were needed to prevent the spread of contagious diseases. Several such conditions, mostly severe skin problems, were referred to as 'leprosy', and two long biblical chapters (Leviticus 13—14) are devoted to diagnosis and prevention of it. Sufferers had to live away from towns and shout 'unclean' to warn others not to approach them (13.45). If they were healed, this had to be certified by a **priest** (14.2–32).

life, soul, spirit

Ancient people held many different views about what made human beings the special creatures they are. Some, including many Jews, believed that to be complete, humans needed bodies as well as inner selves. Others, including many influenced by the philosophy of Plato (fourth century BC), believed that the important part of a human was the 'soul' (Gk: *psyche*), which at death would be happily freed from its bodily prison. Confusingly for us, the same word *psyche* is often used in the New Testament within a Jewish framework where it clearly means 'life' or 'true self', without implying a body/soul dualism that devalues the body. Human inwardness of experience and understanding can also be referred to as 'spirit'. *See also* **resurrection**.

message, *see* good news

Messiah, messianic, Christ

The Hebrew word means literally 'anointed one', hence in theory either a prophet, **priest** or king. In Greek this translates as *Christos*; 'Christ' in early Christianity was a title, and only gradually became an alternative proper name for Jesus. In practice 'Messiah' is mostly restricted to the notion, which took various forms in ancient Judaism, of the coming king who would be David's true heir, through whom YHWH would bring judgment to the world, and in particular would rescue Israel from pagan enemies. There was no single template of expectations. Scriptural stories and promises contributed to different ideals and movements, often focused on (a) decisive military defeat of Israel's enemies and (b) rebuilding or cleansing the **Temple**. The **Dead Sea Scrolls** speak of two 'Messiahs', one a priest and the other a king. The universal early Christian belief that Jesus was Messiah is only explicable, granted his crucifixion by the Romans (which would have been seen as a clear sign that he was not the Messiah), by their belief that God had raised him from the dead, so vindicating the implicit messianic claims of his earlier ministry.

miracles

Like some of the old prophets, notably Elijah and Elisha, Jesus performed many deeds of remarkable power, particularly healings. The **gospels** refer to these as 'deeds of power', 'signs', 'marvels' or 'paradoxes'. Our word 'miracle' tends to imply that God, normally 'outside' the closed system of the world, sometimes 'intervenes'; miracles have then frequently been denied as a matter of principle. However, in the Bible God is always present, however strangely, and 'deeds of power' are seen as *special* acts of a *present* God rather than as *intrusive* acts of an *absent* one. Jesus' own 'mighty works' are seen particularly, following prophecy, as evidence of his messiahship (e.g. Matthew 11.2–6).

Mishnah

The main codification of Jewish law (**Torah**) by the **rabbis**, produced in about AD 200, reducing to writing the 'oral Torah' which in Jesus' day ran parallel to the 'written Torah'. The Mishnah is itself the basis of the much larger collections of traditions in the two Talmuds (roughly AD 400).

parables

From the Old Testament onwards, prophets and other teachers used various storytelling devices as vehicles for their challenge to Israel (e.g. 2 Samuel 12.1–7). Sometimes these appeared as visions with interpretations (e.g. Daniel 7). Similar techniques were used by the **rabbis**. Jesus made his own creative adaptation of these traditions, in order to break open the world-view of his contemporaries and to invite them to share his vision of God's **kingdom** instead. His stories portrayed this as something that was *happening*, not just a timeless truth, and enabled his hearers to step inside the story and make it their own. As with some Old Testament visions, some of Jesus' parables have their own interpretations (e.g. the sower, Mark 4); others are thinly disguised retellings of the prophetic story of Israel (e.g. the wicked tenants, Mark 12).

parousia

Literally, it means 'presence', as opposed to 'absence', and is sometimes used by Paul with this sense (e.g. Philippians 2.12). It was already used in the Roman world for the ceremonial arrival of, for example, the emperor at a subject city or colony. Although the ascended Lord is not 'absent' from the church, when he 'appears' (Colossians 3.4; 1 John 3.2) in his 'second coming' this will be, in effect, an 'arrival' like that of the emperor, and Paul uses it thus in 1 Corinthians 15.23; 1 Thessalonians 2.19; etc. In the **gospels** it is found only in Matthew 24 (vv. 3, 27, 39).

Pharisees, legal experts, lawyers, rabbis

The Pharisees were an unofficial but powerful Jewish pressure group through most of the first centuries BC and AD. Largely lay-led, though including some **priests**, their aim was to purify Israel through intensified observance of the Jewish law (**Torah**), developing their own traditions about the precise meaning and application of scripture, their own patterns of prayer and other devotion, and their own calculations of the national hope. Though not all legal experts were Pharisees, most Pharisees were thus legal experts.

They effected a democratization of Israel's life, since for them the study and practice of Torah was equivalent to worshipping in the **Temple** – though they were adamant in pressing their own rules for the Temple liturgy on an unwilling (and often **Sadducean**) priesthood. This enabled them to survive AD 70 and, merging into the early rabbinic movement, to develop new ways forward. Politically they stood up for ancestral traditions, and were at the forefront of various movements of revolt against both pagan overlordship and compromised Jewish leaders. By Jesus' day there were two distinct schools, the stricter one of Shammai, more inclined towards armed revolt, and the more lenient one of Hillel, ready to live and let live.

Jesus' debates with the Pharisees are at least as much a matter of agenda and policy (Jesus strongly opposed their separatist nationalism) as about details of theology and piety. Saul of Tarsus was a fervent right-wing Pharisee, presumably a Shammaite, until his conversion.

After the disastrous war of AD 66–70, these schools of Hillel and Shammai continued bitter debate on appropriate policy. Following the further disaster of AD 135 (the failed Bar-Kochba revolt against Rome) their traditions were carried on by the rabbis who, though looking to the earlier Pharisees for inspiration, developed a Torah-piety in which personal holiness and purity took the place of political agendas.

present age, age to come, eternal life

By the time of Jesus many Jewish thinkers divided history into two periods: 'the present age' and 'the age to come' – the latter being the time when YHWH would at last act decisively to judge evil, to rescue Israel, and to create a new world of justice and peace. The early Christians believed that, though the full blessings of the coming age lay still in the future, it had already begun with Jesus, particularly with his death and **resurrection**, and that by **faith** and **baptism** they were able to enter it already. 'Eternal life' does not mean simply 'existence continuing without end', but 'the life of the age to come'.

priests, high priest

Aaron, the older brother of Moses, was appointed Israel's first high priest (Exodus 28—29), and in theory his descendants were Israel's priests thereafter. Other members of his tribe (Levi) were 'Levites', performing other liturgical duties but not sacrificing. Priests lived among the people all around the country, having a local teaching role (Leviticus 10.11; Malachi 2.7), and going to Jerusalem by rotation to perform the **Temple** liturgy (e.g. Luke 2.8).

David appointed Zadok (whose Aaronic ancestry is sometimes questioned) as high priest, and his family remained thereafter the senior priests in Jerusalem, probably the ancestors of the **Sadducees**. One explanation of the origins of the **Qumran** Essenes is that they were a dissident group who believed themselves to be the rightful chief priests.

Qumran, see Dead Sea Scrolls

rabbis, see Pharisees

repentance

Literally, this means 'turning back'. It is widely used in the Old Testament and subsequent Jewish literature to indicate both a personal turning away from sin and Israel's corporate turning away from idolatry and back to YHWH. Through both meanings, it is linked to the idea of 'return from **exile**'; if Israel is to 'return' in all senses, it must 'return' to YHWH. This is at the heart of the summons of both **John the Baptist** and Jesus. In Paul's writings it is mostly used for **Gentiles** turning away from idols to serve the true God; also for sinning Christians who need to return to Jesus.

resurrection

In most biblical thought, human bodies matter and are not merely disposable prisons for the **soul**. When ancient Israelites wrestled with the goodness and justice of YHWH, the creator, they ultimately came to insist that he must raise the dead (Isaiah 26.19; Daniel 12.2–3) – a suggestion firmly resisted by classical pagan thought. The longed-for return from **exile** was also spoken of in terms of YHWH raising dry bones to new **life** (Ezekiel 37.1–14). These ideas were developed in the second-**Temple** period, not least at times of martyrdom (e.g. 2 Maccabees 7). Resurrection was not just 'life after death', but a newly embodied life *after* 'life after death'; those at present dead were either 'asleep', or seen as 'souls', 'angels' or 'spirits', awaiting new embodiment.

The early Christian belief that Jesus had been raised from the dead was not that he had 'gone to **heaven**', or that he had been 'exalted', or was 'divine'; they believed all those as well, but each could have been expressed without mention of resurrection. Only the bodily resurrection of Jesus explains the rise of the early church, particularly its belief in Jesus' messiahship (which his crucifixion would have called into question). The early Christians believed that they themselves would be raised to a new, transformed bodily life at the time of the Lord's return or **parousia** (e.g. Philippians 3.20f.).

sabbath

The Jewish sabbath, the seventh day of the week, was a regular reminder both of creation (Genesis 2.3; Exodus 20.8–11) and of the **Exodus** (Deuteronomy 5.15). Along with **circumcision** and the food laws, it was one of the badges of Jewish identity within the pagan world of late antiquity, and a considerable body of Jewish **law** and custom grew up around its observance.

sacrifice

Like all ancient people, the Israelites offered animal and vegetable sacrifices to their God. Unlike others, they possessed a highly detailed written code (mostly in Leviticus) for what to offer and how to offer it; this in turn was developed in the **Mishnah** (*c.* AD 200). The Old Testament specifies that sacrifices can only be offered in the Jerusalem **Temple**; after this was destroyed in AD 70, sacrifices ceased, and Judaism developed further the idea, already present in some teachings, of prayer, fasting and almsgiving as alternative forms of sacrifice. The early Christians used the language of sacrifice in connection with such things as holiness, evangelism and the **eucharist**.

Sadducees

By Jesus' day, the Sadducees were the aristocracy of Judaism, possibly tracing their origins to the family of Zadok, David's **high priest**. Based in Jerusalem, and including most of the leading priestly families, they had their own traditions and attempted to resist the pressure of the **Pharisees** to conform to theirs. They claimed to rely only on the Pentateuch (the first five books of the Old Testament), and denied any doctrine of a future life, particularly of the **resurrection** and other ideas associated with it, presumably because of the encouragement such beliefs gave to revolutionary movements. No writings from the Sadducees have survived, unless the apocryphal book of Ben-Sirach ('Ecclesiasticus') comes from them. The Sadducees themselves did not survive the destruction of Jerusalem and the **Temple** in AD 70.

the satan, 'the accuser', demons

The Bible is never very precise about the identity of the figure known as 'the satan'. The Hebrew word means 'the accuser', and at times the satan seems to be a member of YHWH's heavenly council, with special responsibility as director of prosecutions (1 Chronicles 21.1; Job 1—2; Zechariah 3.1f.). However, it becomes identified variously with the serpent of the garden of Eden (Genesis 3.1–15) and with the rebellious daystar cast out of **heaven** (Isaiah 14.12–15), and was seen by many Jews as the quasi-personal source of evil standing behind both human wickedness and large-scale injustice, sometimes operating through semi-independent 'demons'. By Jesus' time various words were used to denote this figure, including Beelzebul/b (lit. 'Lord of the flies') and simply 'the evil one'; Jesus warned his followers against the deceits this figure could perpetrate. His opponents accused him of being in league with the satan, but the early Christians believed that Jesus in fact defeated it both in his own struggles with temptation (Matthew 4; Luke 4), his exorcisms of demons, and his death (1 Corinthians 2.8; Colossians 2.15). Final victory over this ultimate enemy is thus assured (Revelation 20), though the struggle can still be fierce for Christians (Ephesians 6.10–20).

scribes

In a world where many could not write, or not very well, a trained class of writers ('scribes') performed the important function of drawing up contracts for business, marriage, etc. Many would thus be legal experts, and quite possibly **Pharisees**, though being a scribe was compatible with various political and religious standpoints. The work of Christian scribes was of vital importance in copying early Christian writings, particularly the stories about Jesus.

son of David, David's son

An alternative, and infrequently used, title for **Messiah**. The messianic promises of the Old Testament often focus specifically on David's son, for example 2 Samuel 7.12–16; Psalm 89.19–37. Joseph, Mary's husband, is called 'son of David' by the angel in Matthew 1.20.

son of God

Originally a title for Israel (Exodus 4.22) and the Davidic king (Psalm 2.7); also used of ancient angelic figures (Genesis 6.2). By the New Testament period it was already used as a **messianic** title, for example in the **Dead Sea Scrolls**. There, and when used of Jesus in the **gospels** (e.g. Matthew 16.16), it means, or reinforces, 'Messiah', without the later significance of 'divine'. However, already in Paul the transition to the fuller meaning (one who was already equal with God and was sent by him to become human and to become Messiah) is apparent, without loss of the meaning 'Messiah' itself (e.g. Galatians 4.4).

son of man

In Hebrew or Aramaic, this simply means 'mortal' or 'human being'; in later Judaism, it is sometimes used to mean 'I' or 'someone like me'. In the New Testament the phrase is frequently linked to Daniel 7.13, where 'one like a son of man' is brought on the clouds of **heaven** to 'the Ancient of Days', being vindicated after a period of suffering, and is given kingly power. Though Daniel 7 itself interprets this as code for 'the people of the saints of the Most High', by the first century some Jews understood it as a **messianic** promise. Jesus developed this in his own way in certain key sayings which are best understood as promises that God would vindicate him, and judge those who had opposed him, after his own suffering (e.g. Mark 14.62). Jesus was thus able to use the phrase as a cryptic self-designation, hinting at his coming suffering, his vindication and his God-given authority.

soul, *see* life

spirit, *see* life, holy spirit

Temple

The Temple in Jerusalem was planned by David (*c*. 1000 BC) and built by his son Solomon as the central sanctuary for all Israel. After reforms under Hezekiah and Josiah in the seventh century BC, it was destroyed by Babylon in 587 BC. Rebuilding by the returned **exiles** began in 538 BC, and was completed in 516, initiating the 'second Temple period'. Judas Maccabaeus cleansed it in 164 BC after its desecration by Antiochus Epiphanes (167). Herod the Great began to rebuild and beautify it in 19 BC; the work was completed in AD 63. The Temple was destroyed by the Romans in AD 70. Many Jews believed it should and would be rebuilt; some still do. The Temple was not only the place of **sacrifice**; it was believed to be the unique dwelling of **YHWH** on earth, the place where **heaven** and earth met.

Torah, Jewish law

'Torah', narrowly conceived, consists of the first five books of the Old Testament, the 'five books of Moses' or 'Pentateuch'. (These contain much law, but also much narrative.) It can also be used for the whole Old Testament scriptures, though strictly these are the 'law, prophets and writings'. In a broader sense, it refers to the whole developing corpus of Jewish legal tradition, written and oral; the oral Torah was initially codified in the **Mishnah** around AD 200, with wider developments found in the two Talmuds, of Babylon and Jerusalem, codified around AD 400. Many Jews in the time of Jesus and Paul regarded the Torah as being so strongly God-given as to be almost itself, in some sense, divine; some (e.g. Ben-Sirach 24) identified it with the figure of 'Wisdom'. Doing what Torah said was not seen as a means of earning God's favour, but rather of expressing gratitude, and as a key badge of Jewish identity.

the Twelve, *see* apostle

word, *see* good news

Word

The prologue to John's gospel (1.1–18) uses Word (Greek: *logos*) in a special sense, based on the ancient Israelite view of God's Word in creation and new creation. Here the Word is Jesus, the personal presence of the God who remains other than the world. He is the one through whom creation came into being; he is the one, now, through whom it will be healed and restored.

YHWH

The ancient Israelite name for God, from at least the time of the **Exodus** (Exodus 6.2f.). It may originally have been pronounced 'Yahweh', but by the time of Jesus it was considered too holy to speak out loud, except for the **high priest** once a year in the Holy of Holies in the **Temple**. Instead, when reading scripture, pious Jews would say *Adonai*, 'Lord', marking this usage by adding the vowels of *Adonai* to the consonants of YHWH, eventually producing the hybrid 'Jehovah'.

The word YHWH is formed from the verb 'to be', combining 'I am who I am', 'I will be who I will be', and perhaps 'I am because I am', emphasizing YHWH's sovereign creative power.